The
Joy of Smoking

The Joy of Smoking

the LIGHT-HEARTED LOOK AT LIGHTING UP!

SUE CARROLL
AND
SUE BREALEY

metro

Published by John Blake Publishing Ltd,
3, Bramber Court, 2 Bramber Road,
London W14 9PB, England

www.blake.co.uk

First published in paperback in 2005

ISBN 1 84454 115 0

British Library Cataloguing-in-Publication Data:

A catalogue record for this book is available from the British Library.

Design by www.envydesign.co.uk

Printed in Great Britain by Bookmarque

1 3 5 7 9 10 8 6 4 2

Papers used by John Blake Publishing are natural, recyclable products made
from wood grown in sustainable forests. The manufacturing processes
conform to the environmental regulations of the country of origin.

Every attempt has been made to contact the relevant copyright-holders, but
some were unobtainable. We would be grateful if the appropriate people
could contact us.

All content contained within this book is for information and entertainment
only. The publisher does not support or endorse the act of smoking and
acknowledges that smoking is harmful.

To our parents and to all Sue Carroll's wonderful and long-suffering friends who've put up with her puffing for the last 30 years (and, no, she's not going to give up...)

ACKNOWLEDGEMENTS

The authors wish to thank Greg Bennett at the *Mirror*, and Fagtags.com for kind permission to reproduce their anarchic labels in this book.

WHEN YOU STOP SMOKING YOU WILL:

1. Get fat
2. Develop the mood swings of a menopausal woman, even if you're a man
3. Stay home and cry
4. Lose your friends
5. Cough
6. Ponder the meaning of life (without a cigarette)
7. Decide it's not worth living
8. Discover a manic desire to chew things, sometimes carpets
9. Realise every penny saved has gone on patches and gum
10. Finally realise, after standing downwind of smokers, that passive smoking is a myth
11. Wonder what it is that hands are actually for
12. Punish yourself at the gym or indulge in some other form of self-flagellation because this is the 'new' you
13. Cry some more
14. Seek therapy
15. Take a nostalgic trip to the smoking room
16. Buy a packet of cigarettes
17. Hide packet of cigarettes
18. Sniff packet of cigarettes
19. Smoke packet of cigarette
20. Find life is worth living again

CONTENTS

INTRODUCTION

No one's allowed to smoke, or tell a dirty joke,
and whistling is forbidden
If chewing gum is chewed, the chewer is pursued,
and in the hoosegow hidden
If any form of pleasure is exhibited, report to me,
and it shall be prohibited
I'll put my foot down, so shall it be, this is the
land of the free.

So sings Groucho, cigar in hand, as Rufus T Firefly, Leader of Freedonia in the 1933 Marx Brothers classic *Duck Soup*. It was supposed to be a joke, but in today's healthist society, where everyone is expected to do their duty by living for a hundred years, it's fast becoming a hellish reality.

Were you to believe the prophets of doom, there's very little in everyday life that doesn't pose a serious threat to our health, indeed, our very existence. Beef burgers, coffee, red wine, white wine (actually, just write off alcohol completely), electric blankets, weed killer, barbecues, salmon, sunshine, rain, HRT patches, butter, bread, garden forks. The list is endless.

But aren't there a couple of things missing? Ah yes, tobacco and the weak and irresponsible smoker, both under attack from the self-righteous 'ban public smoking' crowd. Well, smokers know the bad news, thank you. Read the book, seen those horrible ads on TV and bought the T-shirt. And, in case smokers haven't quite got the picture, there are warnings slapped on every fag packet (not to mention a massive tax).

Indeed, the smoker is not only endangering himself, but also an ever-increasing list of innocent victims. Ignoring the fact that a morning stroll through Glasgow is the equivalent of smoking a packet of fags, thousands of spurious statistics are reeled out every week about the danger of passive smoking. Has anyone conclusively proved, amid all the hysteria, how many cigarettes are 'passively' smoked by abstainers? And at least you get more conversation from someone puffing their way through a pack of twenty than from the exhaust of an HGV.

Our aim is not to get too angry with the smoke fascists, but to display the tolerance they, the greatest killjoys since Oliver Cromwell and his band of

Puritans, deny us. We won't dwell (too much) on the fact that their sanctimonious nagging gets as much up our noses as our smoke gets in their eyes. Or what might, or might not, happen in Britain over the next few years. After all, we've witnessed the abject misery of outlawed smokers in America, especially in California where, ludicrously, cigarettes are banned on public beaches. It's all too depressing. Let's puff on while we've still got the chance.

So what we'll tell you instead is that, contrary to current thinking, the non-smoker has existed for centuries alongside the smoker. In fact, this book is a collaboration between a cigarette fiend (Sue C) and someone who has never lit up in her life (Sue B), though admittedly there have been opponents to the weed. Hitler was evangelical about his loathing for tobacco and launched the very first anti-smoking advertising campaign. Need we say more?

Well, yes, actually, we do.

No amount of carping or moralising can alter one simple fact. Those who continue to smoke do so because they enjoy it. Writer and former smoker Beryl Bainbridge once said that ciggies are 'a comfort to the soul', and she's right. But there is something else: the pleasure and fellowship of belonging to the society of smokers, a club that faces the prospect of being all but driven underground, yet, to the fury of the smoke-haters, continues to flourish.

We choose to smoke because we can: free will and individual choice are the foundations of any civilised society and must be defended. As we see our rights eroded on a daily basis, it has never been more vital to remain dogged in the determination to maintain our civil liberties and resist the persecutors.

In the course of researching this book we've unearthed some fascinating facts about tobacco, tapped a source of amazing anecdotes and found some truly colourful characters. The enduring thread is the unity of smokers, their shared philosophy on life and unfailing sense of humour. Smokers form the largest minority group in the world and that's really something to celebrate. We reckon this book will cost you about the same as a pack of twenty. And we know it will bring you as much pleasure.

It's been a joy to write.

CHAPTER ONE

UP IN SMOKE: A BRIEF ROMP THROUGH THE HISTORY OF TOBACCO

Smoking chills

Christopher Columbus, Sir Water Raleigh and Sir Francis Drake have all been blamed (or credited, depending on your point of view) with introducing the much-maligned weed to Europe.

Wrong.

Columbus did indeed receive a present of fruit and tobacco from the Arawak Indians the day he discovered the New World in 1492. But, as soon as he was out of sight, he ate the fruit and chucked the dried leaves overboard. Two weeks later he reached Cuba, where members of an expedition sent inland reported the strange sight of natives 'with a little lighted brand made from a kind of plant whose aroma it was their custom to inhale'. One of these explorers, Rodrigo de Jerez, determined to immerse himself in the local custom, and ended up chain-smoking his way back across the Atlantic. By the time Columbus reached Spain in March 1493, de Jerez was hooked and, before you could say 'nicotine', was joined by thousands of his countrymen in this strangely compelling habit.

FACT
One of the earliest methods of consuming tobacco was as a tea that was 'drunk' through the nose or via the anus.

But not all were seduced by the weed. The military governor of Hispaniola, Gonzalo Fernadez de Oviedo, gave one of the first anti-tobacco rants on record: 'Among other evil practices, the Indians have one that is especially harmful: the ingestion of a certain kind of smoke they call tobacco. They imbibe the smoke until they become unconscious and lie sprawling on the ground like men in a drunken stupor … It seems to me that here we have a bad and pernicious custom.'

Poor Gonzalo. All that disgust and indignation was to no avail, as the European lust for tobacco proved insatiable. In 1531, large-scale cultivation of the weed began in Santo Domingo and by the end of the century commercial crops were growing in Cuba and Brazil.

In the meantime, word had spread to other European courts whose monarchs, wishing to be at the cutting edge of new developments, dispatched lackeys to obtain this exciting new substance. One of these, Jean Nicot, snaffled some of the tobacco cuttings destined for his master, Henri II of France, and began to explore some of the plant's legendary medicinal benefits. After he claimed to have cured a man of a tumour with an ointment made from tobacco leaves, the 'Nicotian Herb' was taken up by

3

the French court and found to be irresistible. Nicotine was born.

> **FACT**
> A single tobacco seed is all but invisible. One million seeds would weigh barely three ounces.

To the French, nicotine was useful in combating illness and disease, everything from worms to toothache. To the English, it represented pleasure, and it was in Elizabethan England that tobacco smoking became an activity of mass appeal rather than a distraction enjoyed only by the elite. When buccaneer and people's darling Francis Drake was given 'feathers and bags of tobacco' by friendly natives in what is now San Francisco, he did not jettison his gifts but carried the precious cargo home to his queen and countrymen. It is also known that Sir Walter Raleigh, cloak-laying favourite of Elizabeth I, brought back tobacco from his first Virginian expedition in 1586, and it was he who persuaded his mistress to sample the delights of tobacco. Gloriana was captivated by the habit, thus ensuring its fashionable take-up among nobility and common folk alike.

Having adopted the custom directly from North American Indians, the English chose the pipe as the preferred implement for taking in smoke, rather than the cigar favoured by the Spanish. Members of the nobility appointed special servants, employed solely to trail around after them carrying their pipes, tobacco and many other implements needed to light up. The hoi polloi made do with a tiny clay pipe and a hot coal, but no matter. The result was very much the same, that of 'pleasing drunkenness'. In 1598, a German visitor to London noted: 'The English are constantly smoking the Nicotian weed. They draw the smoke into their mouths, which they puff out again through their nostrils, like funnels, along with it plenty of phlegm and defluxion from the head.' At this time tobacco cost £4.10s per pound; a flagon of ale cost a penny.

Tobacco's expense was partly due to the fact that the English, as yet, had no plantations abroad and therefore no direct access to the weed. Tobacco enthusiasts relied largely for their supply on Drake and his swashbuckling mates, who ambushed foreign ships travelling from the New World and commandeered their precious cargo. Raleigh, the weed's greatest champion of the age, planted tobacco alongside his other great discovery, the potato, at his estate in Ireland, where he was promptly relieved of it by a bunch of thieving locals. They left the potatoes, though.

Every schoolboy knows the story that on one occasion Sir Water Raleigh, while smoking, was doused in water by a well-meaning servant who thought he was on fire. Fewer will know that Raleigh became the first to enlist tobacco as the dying man's comfort. As he ascended the scaffold in 1618, the victim of a trumped-up charge brought by the puritanical King James I, Raleigh ran his finger across the blade of the axe and commented with a smile, 'This is sharp medicine but it will cure all disease.' He insisted on smoking to the last, and kept his pipe in his mouth until his head fell. The contrast between the witty, pioneering Elizabethan and the dour, anti-smoking Jacobean could not be starker.

> **FACT**
> Sir Walter Raleigh's pipe box carried the inscription: 'It was my companion in that most wretched time', a reference to his years in jail under King James I.

Meanwhile, the cultivators of tobacco in the Americas had not been idle and their ranks were swelled daily by Englishmen unable to live with James's canting ways. In 1612, John Rolfe planted some *Nicotiana tabacum* seeds in Virginia and set about learning the art of cultivation, harvesting and curing the delicate plant. In this he was helped by the family of his wife, the Indian princess Pocahontas who had captured his attention by performing naked cartwheels in front of him. Thanks to the skills of his in-laws, Rolfe succeeded in creating a tobacco with a unique taste and aroma, which immediately found favour in the English market. Despite the King's entrenched opposition in England, such was demand that tobacco shipments to London went from 20,000 pounds in 1618 to 1.5 million pounds in 1627. At the time of James's death there were 7,000 establishments selling tobacco in London alone.

All was not plain sailing, however. Life expectancy for English colonists was just six months and tobacco cultivation was a labour-intensive occupation. Then, in 1619, a ship arrived in Chesapeake Bay and John Rolfe recorded a momentous event in his diary: 'There came in a Dutch man-of-warre that sold us 20 negars.' The cheap source of manpower was seized on eagerly by the colonists and marked the beginning of the slave trade. The Chesapeake became the largest tobacco producer in the world and by 1700 was exporting 38 million pounds of the weed to Britain, a rise of nearly 60,000 per cent on its 1620 levels.

The story was much the same in the rest of Europe. The Spanish smoked everywhere, at play and at prayer, only desisting when Pope Urban VIII threatened to excommunicate anyone caught smoking in a holy place. The Thirty Years War saw the start of tobacco as the soldier's friend and the spread of the weed to Sweden and Holland, where it had hitherto been relatively unknown. But, as ever, tobacco had its detractors. 'I cannot refrain from a few words of protest against the fashion lately introduced from America,' sniffed a horrified German visitor, 'a sort of smoke tippling … which enslaves its victims more completely than any other form of intoxication, old or new. These madmen will swallow or inhale with incredible eagerness the smoke of a plant they call Herba Nicotina, or tobacco.'

Tobacco was the new hot ticket and the resourceful Dutch recognised that it possessed a currency value that was global, giving it infinite possibilities as an instrument of trade. In 1652 they bought the entire Cape of Good Hope for 'a certain quantity of tobacco and brandy'. The Dutch became the main traffickers of the weed throughout the world, creating new, enthusiastic markets wherever they took this wonderful habit.

In England, the smokers had survived the unwelcome attentions of James I and his son Charles I (who was determined to outdo his father in the unpopularity stakes and was beheaded for his pains) and the tuttings of the tight-lipped Puritans. Charles II had one brief go at burning the tobacco fields at Winchcombe in Gloucestershire, and came to the wise conclusion that he was literally playing with fire. His subjects chain-smoked throughout the great plague of 1665, believing that tobacco had medicinal and preventative qualities, but they hardly needed the Black Death as an excuse for lighting up. Another visitor from the Continent was flabbergasted to observe that, 'In England, when the children went to school, they carried in their satchels, with their books, a pipe of tobacco, which their mothers took care to fill early in the morning, it serving them instead of a breakfast.'

> **FACT**
> 'This morning I got together 36 horse and found an armed multitude guarding the tobacco field ... a rabble of men and women calling for blood for the tobacco. The soldiers stood firm, and with cocked pistols, bade the multitude disperse but they would not, and 200 more came from Winchcombe. Ten men could not in four days destroy the good tobacco about Cheltenham ... I was forced to retreat.'
> Letter from a government agent, 1658

North of the border, the Scots were playing catch-up. The country that gave birth to the weed-hating King James viewed the English obsession with tobacco as sinful and excessive, and William Barclay of Towie exhorted his countrymen 'not, as the English abusers do, to make a smoke box of their skulls'. But in 1707 England and Scotland became one country and within 15 years the Scots were controlling 50 per cent of the tobacco trade. They tore down the Glaswegian fishing huts and replaced them with vast tobacco wharves, superbly placed to exploit the shipping routes to the tobacco plantations of the New World. Such was their domination and understanding of the market that, when the American War of Independence caused a major tobacco shortage in Britain, the Scots had already stockpiled huge quantities in anticipation. Prices soared from 3p per pound to 38p and drove the English to reintroduce the cultivation of home-grown baccy in Yorkshire.

But their problems were nothing compared to those of the French peasantry, whose tax on tobacco was twice that of their British equivalents. If life wasn't exactly a picnic for tillers of the soil in Britain, for the average French yokel it was a life of unremitting poverty and grind, relieved only by the occasional smoke. What's more, the weed's ability to suppress appetite was especially useful in a world where there was never enough to eat. The French ruling classes had supported the American colonists against their British overlords. Now they were to pay the price as the *sans-culottes* turned on their masters with a hatred that inspired an orgy of blood-letting. Snuff, inextricably linked with the aristocracy, went out of fashion overnight, and snuffers with any sense switched to smoking with all speed. In the hysterical frenzy of denouncements and executions that followed the revolution, an impromptu sneezing fit was all it took to finish up on the guillotine.

For the first two years of the Republic, the French rejoiced in the fact that they were the only citizens in Europe to enjoy tax-free tobacco, only to have this enviable status cut abruptly short by the infamous pocket-sized tyrant, Napoleon Bonaparte. Just one generation after the execution of Louis XVI and his cake-eating queen Marie Antoinette, the little Corsican had introduced a punitive tobacco tax to fund his megalomaniacal military ambitions and was generating more income from tobacco than any of his high-born predecessors had dreamed of. By the time he finished rearranging the map of Europe, he had created a greater demand for tobacco than ever before.

> **FACT**
> Napoleon Bonaparte had a kilo-a-week snuff
> habit, the equivalent to 100 ciggies a day.

Just as, 200 hundred years earlier, the Thirty Years War
had occasioned a huge surge in demand for tobacco,
the Napoleonic Wars were to do the same, opening up
the vast Russian market to the weed. Compared to the
rest of Europe, smoking had not captured the Russian
imagination and smoking had been confined to the
Russian aristocracy, who imbibed through enormous,
exotic hookahs. As these were less than practical for
battlefield use, the new nico-converts found other
methods of smoking, including cigars, a habit that had
found its way from Spain. Yet again, tobacco was
discovered to have an essential role as an appetite
suppressant among troops suffering extreme food
deprivation, not to mention its calming properties
in the face of battle. No wonder that the weed has
become known as the 'Patron Saint of Soldiers'.

Elsewhere, the now legendary camaraderie
between boozers and smokers became apparent, as
French and British soldiers used brief lulls in
hostilities to trade tobacco and brandy off the field.
But it was the British who were to triumph on the
field, and Napoleon was exiled to St Helena, one of

the tiniest islands in the South Atlantic, where the British taxpayer funded his snuffing habit for the remainder of his days. The Duke of Wellington and the army that he referred to as 'scum' returned home victorious to a nation more in love with tobacco than ever before, and a new method of smoking the delicious weed. Fifteen years before Waterloo, Britain imported just 26 pounds of cigars. Fifteen years after the battle, imports rocketed to more than 250,000 pounds, an increase of nearly one million per cent, and tobacconists sprang up all over Britain to exploit this phenomenon.

FACT
'The best judge of an Havana cigar' in the 1830s was considered to be one Charles Lambert who, along with a Mr Butler, ran a tobacconist in Drury Lane.

Smoking became a feature of everyday life, made even more joyous by the appearance of the friction match in 1850 and the cigarette six years later. This ingenious little tobacco stick was an innovation of the Turks and enthusiastically taken up by their British allies during the Crimean War, where, for the first time (but not the last), it became the soldier's solace. Some disapproved, seeing the cigarette as 'a miserable apology for a manly pleasure', but, seeing its potential, returning war veteran Robert Peacock Gloag began to turn out handmade cigarettes in 1856, followed closely by Bond Street tobacconist Philip Morris.

At first a sideline, the cigarette quickly gained a huge following in the tobacco market and, across the Atlantic, American consumption shot up from 42 million cigarettes in 1875 to 500 million in just five years. Manufacturers couldn't roll out handmade cigarettes fast enough to meet demand. Not only that, the wages of the rollers accounted for a whopping 90 per cent of the production costs. Tobacco giants Allen & Ginter came up with the novel idea of offering a prize of $75,000 to anyone who could find a way of improving production. One bright young spark came up with the Bonsack machine, which rolled out 70,000 ciggies a day. In a move smacking of lunacy, A&G refused to cough up the prize money, and the marvellous machine was snapped up by James 'Buck' Duke, the owner of a tiny Virginian tobacco company. The Duke splashed out a massive 20 per cent of his turnover on advertising, introduced collectable cigarette cards and installed agents at the docks to hand out

14

Duke cigarettes to immigrants as they landed. His enterprise and aggressive tactics paid off – within five years he was selling 2 million cigarettes a day.

> **FACT**
> **The famous card sharp 'Poker Alice' Tubbs (1851–1930) refused to be converted to the cigarette and died at the age of 79 after a lifetime's love affair with cigars.**

Suddenly cigarettes were the hip thing, while pipes were passé for the very reason that they *couldn't* be passed around at social gatherings, one of the great attractions of the ciggie. Cigarettes had an air of conviviality: they could be shared around and used to effect introductions. But above all they were perceived as glamorous and smoked by elegant people. They symbolised everything a person wanted to be, confident, alluring, irresistible, with a hint of danger.

America smoked everything that the Bonsack machines threw at them, and the market for cigarettes appeared infinite. 'Buck' Duke had by far the largest share of the market, but that wasn't enough for him, he wanted the whole cake. Superbly placed to achieve this, he started swallowing up small competitors, (including the unfortunate Allen & Ginter), raised his spend on advertising even further and introduced a ruthless pricing strategy. The other manufacturers ran up the white flag and sued for peace on Buck's terms. In 1889, what was left of the opposition was gobbled up into the American Tobacco Company, with the 33-year-old Duke as its president.

Then, in 1896, the unthinkable happened. Cigarette consumption fell and continued to fall. Duke needed new markets and, seeing that the Old Country had a heck of a lot of smokers, he turned his sales and marketing talents on the British, who unfortunately proved unresponsive both to his price cuts and the black arts of advertising. Undeterred, he got on the next ocean liner bound for Europe to give the Brits the full force of the Duke personality first-hand. To show he meant business, he began buying up small regional manufacturers. But the British had not painted a third of the world red by allowing an upstart American to steal their business from under their nose. The ten largest manufacturers combined to form the Imperial Tobacco Company and began buying up retailers which, unsurprisingly, refused to stock Duke's brand of cigarettes. This time it was Duke who sued for peace and a new, jointly owned company, British American Tobacco, was set up to exploit the global tobacco market. The first multinational was born.

> *'He found a tree that had not been damaged by shellfire and sat down beneath it, lighting a cigarette and sucking in the smoke. Before the war he had never touched tobacco; now it was his greatest comfort.'*
>
> Birdsong, *Sebastian Faulks*

After a five-year dip in its fortunes, tobacco hit record-breaking levels again in 1901, with China alone consuming 1.25 billion cigarettes a year. But it was the two devastating world wars that altered the course of tobacco and its role in society. Boredom, fear, nerves, hunger, camaraderie, for any number of reasons cigarettes transcended country, cause and no-man's-land to become a source of comfort to both sides. A creeping reluctance to smoke cigarettes had appeared before the war, but, faced with ceaseless shelling, the mud, the rats and the insane waste of life, cigarettes became one of the few symbols of humanity to be had in the hell of the trenches.

Tobacco's importance in maintaining morale was summed up in 1917 when the USA entered the war. General John Pershing, commander of the American Expeditionary Force, observed, 'You ask me what we need to win this war, I answer tobacco, as much as bullets. We must have thousands of tons of it without delay.' His request was granted, with Camels and Lucky Strike being the favourites of the American troops and Woodbines the choice of the British. Troops developed a new way of smoking, with the lit end facing into the palm, so that the glow did not mark them out as a sniper's target. Few who went into the First World War as a non-smoker came out one.

> *Pack up your troubles in your old kit bag*
> *And smile, smile, smile*
> *While you've a lucifer to light your fag*
> *Smile, boys, that's the style.*
> *What's the use of worrying?*
> *It never was worthwhile.*
> *So, pack up your troubles in your old kit bag*
> *And smile, smile, smile.*
>
> *First World War song*

When the mentally and physically scarred war heroes returned to Britain in 1918, few still dismissed cigarettes as 'a miserable apology for a manly pleasure'. What's more, the cigarette had acquired a new and lucrative market via the conflict. It had become increasingly apparent that the support and co-operation of women were essential to achieving victory. War gave British women what militant suffrage had not, the vote and some equality with men, and the cigarette allowed them a public, not to mention delicious, demonstration of their hard-fought victory. Cigarettes now accounted for the majority of tobacco sales, and by 1928 the USA was producing 100 billion cigarettes a year to satisfy demand. Even the Wall Street Crash and the subsequent Great Depression did nothing to halt the triumphant rise of tobacco and its cost. Those who could not afford the inflated prices charged by the tobacco companies picked fag butts off the street to enable themselves to carry on indulging their habit. In 1930, the tobacco historian Count Conti remarked, 'A glance at the statistics proves convincingly that the non-smokers are a feeble and ever dwindling minority.' Smoking crossed the barriers of age, sex and class, as demonstrated by Eleanor Roosevelt who, as the First Lady of the United States of America, delighted smokers everywhere by lighting a cigar in public.

At the start of World War II, President Franklin D Roosevelt made tobacco a protected crop as part of the war effort, and the popular practice of inserting collectable cigarette cards in packets was discontinued to save paper. As the war developed into a truly global conflict, cigarettes were declared essential wartime material. The Yanks further

Field Marshall Montgomery to Sir Winston Churchill: 'I do not drink, I do not smoke. I sleep a great deal. That is why I am 100 per cent fit.'

Churchill to Montgomery: 'I drink a great deal. I sleep little, and I smoke cigar after cigar. That is why I am 200 per cent fit.'

inflamed the grumblings of the British soldiers that they were 'over-sexed, over-paid and over here' by receiving a much larger cigarette allowance than their allies. So internationally widespread had the smoking habit become that spies had to be taught in detail how to smoke in the manner of the country to which they were sent. The smallest mistake could blow an otherwise painstakingly constructed cover.

Cigarettes became the black market's most valuable currency, and it was the only commodity in post-war Germany that was to retain its value. There was nothing that cigarettes could not buy, especially as they had the obvious advantage of only being usable once. A carton of American cigarettes laid out properly could buy anything from a fur coat to a camera, not to mention a little cheap love from a half-starved girl. It was the old story of supply and demand, and in the ruins of the Third Reich there was little of the former and a great deal of the latter. Once again, war had done for cigarettes what a million adverts could not accomplish. A huge number of people, soldiers and civilians alike, had taken up smoking during the conflict, prompted in no small measure by the glamorous escapism offered by their idols on the silver screen, whether in battle or the bedroom. Health concerns about tobacco had been forgotten: the only serious research on such matters had been done by the Nazis, and no one was taking too much notice of their opinions at the time.

FACT
In 1949, Britain had the highest percentage of smokers in the world: 81 per cent of all men smoked, and 39 per cent of women.

However, as the Fifties approached, the ground-breaking work begun by the Third Reich scientists was picked up by a British scientist, Richard Doll. In 1949, Doll produced findings that suggested smoking was linked to lung cancer, but only in 1957 did the government ask for advice based on further research he had carried out. Shortly afterwards, one of the first tobacco lawsuits was brought by a smoker in the USA, who died of cancer during the case. In his absence the jury found he had been killed by lung cancer caused by Lucky Strike cigarettes, but a retrial exonerated the company. Nevertheless, by order of a federal act, on 1 January 1966 cigarette packets began to carry the warning 'Cigarette smoking may be hazardous to your health'. It seemed that no one quite believed it, though, the year saw a rise of 7.8 billion in US ciggie sales. What's more, the century was soon to offer up another major war, timed beautifully to boost tobacco's sales and image. Who cared about government health warnings on cigarette packets when you were a terrified rookie in the hell of Vietnam, especially when the fags were being supplied freely by the people behind the deadly cautions?

FACT
Chairman Mao chain-smoked 'Double Happiness' cigarettes throughout his Cultural Revolution, during which 30 million Chinese starved to death.

At about the time the US government was putting warnings on American cigarette packets, Prime Minister Harold Wilson was named Britain's 'Pipe Smoker of the Year' and The Beatles were swinging their MBEs in one hand with a fag in the other. But in both countries tobacco's glory days were reaching an end. Throughout the Seventies the anti-smoking movement grew in influence and zeal, with non-smokers demanding their rights to 'clean air' in the form of segregated smoking establishments. The first nationwide 'Great American Smokeout' was held in 1977, to persuade smokers to give up their fags and donate the money saved to charity, and a burgeoning industry developed in the shape of counsellors and self-help books to aid the errant smoker in kicking his or her habit. In Britain, government money was made available for the creation of the anti-smoking organisation ASH (Action on Smoking and Health), and for research showing that smoking was responsible for just about every death on the planet. The relentless attacks bore fruit, as in the early Eighties the percentage of male smokers had dropped below 40 per cent, and a survey revealed that the average smoker had been made to feel thoroughly ashamed of himself and his addiction to the weed.

But there still remained a hard core of puffers who, despite being continually bombarded with smoking fatality statistics, simply refused to be slapped into shape by the anti-tobacco brigade. Whatever pathetic underclass the likes of ASH and its followers considered the smoker to inhabit, there was still the matter of that little thing called freedom, which so many smokers had fought so hard to defend throughout the centuries. After all, whose life was it anyway? The answer to the anti-smokers' prayers appeared in the form of ETS, or 'Environmental Tobacco Smoke', that's passive smoking to you. No more was the smoker simply an inadequate and feeble-minded victim of a filthy habit, he was harming others too. The anti-smokers could throw off accusations that they were interfering busybodies and killjoys. Their role was to protect the innocent and defenceless from the selfish smoker.

FACT
A smokeless cigarette called Premier was
released in the USA in May 1988.

Yet although the anti-smoking movement has undoubtedly gained ground, with smoking banned on all forms of public transport and in the work place, it has failed to prove conclusively that smoking kills non-smokers. In 1997, a massive study of 250,000 people, by the American Cancer Society, failed to establish a link between passive smoking and lung cancer. Even more embarrassing was a report, reluctantly published in 1998 by the World Health Organisation, showing that passive smoking could even have a protective effect. *Unsurprisingly*, an ASH spokesman called the findings 'surprising'.

And, while cigarette smoking has declined significantly over the last few decades, it hasn't all gone the antis' way. In 1996, smoking amongst British women rose for the first time in 25 years, and a staggering 56 billion cigarettes are still smoked by Brits every year. Cigar sales are actually on the increase.

Perhaps the final word on the subject should go to the world's wisest and greatest playwright. Shakespeare never made mention of the weed in any of his works – no character smokes it or refers to it – but in his dark play 'Measure for Measure' the rogue Lucio says "it is impossible to extirp it quite, till eating and drinking be put down." He was, in fact, talking about sex, but it might just as well have been tobacco. As long as there are people to eat, drink and draw breath, there will be smokers.

VARIATIONS OF THE WORD TOBACCO: The weed, snuff, maccabooy, plug of tobacco, quid, fid, twist, flake, shag, cigar, cheroot, smoke, cigarette, coffin-nail, reefer, joint, tobacco-pipe, churchwarden, briar, tab, fag, snout, rollies, baccy, sotweed, bidi.

A 'fag end' was the coarser part of a cloth that hangs loose, and came to be applied to the last and poorest part of anything. It was first used to describe inferior cigarettes about 1883.

CHAPTER TWO

INHALE AND EXPIRE: THE HEALTH HYSTERICS AND THEIR IRON FIST OF LOVE

Smoking can aid weight loss as part of a calorie controlled diet

> *Your body belongs to the nation*
> *Your body belongs to the Führer*
> *You have the duty to be healthy*
> *Food is not a private matter.*
>
> German National Socialist Slogan, 1937

Prora was the Third Reich's answer to Butlins, a two-mile-long line of giant accommodation blocks, designed to keep Hans and Lotte fit, productive and co-operative cogs in the Nazi machinery.

'Only sleep should be provided as free time,' shrieked Robert Ley, head of the 'Strength Through Joy' movement, for which Prora was built. 'Organising one's free time on a private basis ... has no sense of value for the German people.'

And he wasn't kidding. The intention was to cram 'holidaymakers' together like sardines and harangue them continuously through loudspeakers, instructing them to fill every waking hour with communal gymnastics, hikes and games. Ley's vision was one of 500,000 German men, women and children aligned in perfectly square ranks as far as the eye could see.

Seventy years on, and thank God for the vigilance of our own health supremacy groups, working overtime to ensure that the nation will be healthy at all costs. Their call for a ban on smoking in public places is just the beginning. It is not only smoking's feeble-minded adherents who must be made to worship at the altar of public health. Drinkers, fatties, pill-poppers, meat-eaters, well, everybody really, must all be made to behave. As everything worth doing, eating, drinking and smoking is rolled into one big target for petty bullying and state intervention, the rest of us look morosely to a future where all choice has been abolished and life isn't worth living.

Daily we are offered the prospect of healthy immortality by being force-fed the latest junk science (sorry, '*health* news') from experts, and let's face it, who isn't an expert these days? Surely the words most calculated to strike weariness into the heart are 'Research suggests', 'Experts fear', 'A clampdown is announced', 'Linked with' and 'A New Study reveals … '

It usually goes like this. Some piece of half-baked research is trotted out as an authoritative fact under an obligatory scare-mongering headline, only to be disproved the next day. A 'study' from the food-savvy denizens claims that soya can prevent cancer. No, wait, it's useless. Staying in the shade can increase the risk of cancer. Oh no, so can going out in the sun. Red wine can 'cut risk of cancer'. No, scrap that too. Wine drinking can cause 'brain damage and memory loss'.

Or what about this little gem from the *Cincinnati Enquirer*: 'Smell of Baked Bread may be Health Hazard'. Quite rightly, the Smokers Club Inc. has sprung into action, demanding an immediate 300 per cent tax on all bread, the banning of all bread advertising within 1,000 feet of a school and the introduction of a new government campaign for teenagers: 'Just Say No to Bread'.

Drawing on more ludicrous stories, statistics and prize research, this chapter explores the extent to which the hysterics will go to make us all part of their health nirvana. Here are a few of our favourites, but BE WARNED. Fish, toast, mushrooms, potatoes and white rice are all killers. Unless you're prepared to live out the rest of your life like a hermit on a fast, your chances of survival are less than great.

ALCOHOL

Wine can cause brain damage

Social drinkers risk brain damage similar to that seen in chronic alcoholics, scientists warned yesterday. Drinking two pints of lager or three glasses of wine a day can lead to memory loss, poor balance and impaired mental agility, researchers found. The findings are particularly worrying as they suggest the 'danger zone' is very close to the recommended limits for 'sensible' drinking advised by the government. Heavy social drinkers were defined as men who drank 60 pints of beer a month (about two a day) and women, 16 bottles of wine a month (three glasses a day). Peter Martin, of Vanderbilt University in Tennessee, who led the research, said, 'Socially functioning heavy drinkers often do not recognise that their level of drinking constitutes a problem that warrants treatment.'

Daily Mail, 16 April 2004

Light drinking helps liver to recover

A couple of drinks a day can help to repair a damaged liver, according to research published yesterday. A study by Dr Gerald Minuk of the University of Manitoba in Canada, who has spent years getting rats drunk, indicates that light drinking is better for the liver than no drinking at all.

Daily Telegraph, 9 November 1999

Wine drinking can 'cut risk of cancer'

Two or three glasses of wine a day can significantly reduce the risk of cancer, according to the biggest survey of the effects of wine consumption upon health. Dr Serge Renaud, who studied the lifestyles of 34,000 men from eastern France between 1978 and 1993, said that those who drank regularly but moderately had a 30 per cent lower mortality rate than teetotallers or heavy drinkers. He said cases of cancer among moderate drinkers fell by 20 per cent compared with other groups, while incidents of heart attacks and brain haemorrhages dropped by 20 to 30 per cent.

Daily Telegraph, 20 February 1998

Cancer risk in a beer a day

People who drink more than seven pints of beer a week are three times more at risk from cancer of the pancreas, according to a report in the *International Journal of Cancer*.

Guardian, 5 April 1989

Home office adviser links youth drinking with Aids

A dangerous link exists between youth drinking and the spread of Aids which must be broken, the Chairwoman of the Home Office working group on young people and alcohol, Lady Masham, claimed yesterday, 'The young socialise in pubs. There's alcohol, then there's sex, then there's Aids.'

Guardian, 26 October 1988

BREAST IMPLANTS

Study questions breast implant risks

Women who have breast enlargements tend to engage in many activities that involve health risks, researchers say. They may drink more, have more sex partners, get pregnant younger and they are more likely to have abortions, use the pill and dye their hair, all factors that researchers should consider when studying the health risk of breast implants, a study said. For example, hair dye could increase the risk of connective tissue diseases while oral contraceptives may increase the risk of arthritis. Failing to consider those factors could conceal the risk arising from breast implants, the study said.
Associated Press, Chicago, 28 May 1997

CANDLES

Devout Catholics 'risk lung cancer'

Church goers risk lung cancer because of unhealthy air caused by candles and incense, researchers say. The scientists found new forms of 'free radicals' that could threaten Roman Catholic rituals. Most at risk would be priests and those who work in churches but 'worshippers devout enough to spend several hours in church' could also be affected, the scientists say. After nine hours of candle burning, the atmosphere in the Roman Catholic basilica in Maastricht, Holland had readings between 12 and 20 times higher than European clean air guidelines. The air quality was worse than in an area used by 45,000 vehicles a day.

Daily Telegraph, 20 November 2004

Candles now blamed for Earth's pollution

Candles are now being blamed for global pollution problems. Burning candles can lead to high levels of pollutants, called particulates, released into the atmosphere. Research by the US Environmental Protection Agency shows the pollution from a burning candle can exceed standards the agency sets outside for outdoor air quality.

www.ananova.com, 14 June 2001

CARS

Perils in the smoke

After completing tests in the Marylebone Road, a report has found that walking in big cities is the equivalent of smoking a cigarette every two and a half minutes. Experts say that pollution kills 40,000 Britons a year.

Daily Express, 12 November 2003

CHEMICALS

The toxic cocktail in our bodies

Britons are contaminated by a toxic cocktail of banned chemicals, a chilling study has revealed. Exposure to dangerous man-made chemicals has left us carrying pesticides, flame retardants and plastics in our bodies. Some have been linked to cancer, infertility, immune system disorders and neurological problems. The environmental group Worldwide Fund for Nature took blood samples from 155 volunteers from 13 UK cities, and analysis by Lancaster University found that every person was contaminated.

Daily Mail, 25 November 2003

How clean-living might be the death of our children

Our desire for a clean home could be the death of us, scientists have warned. Potentially toxic chemicals in household products like air freshener, furniture polish, fabric softener and even non-stick pans have been linked to allergies, breathing difficulties and depression. A study revealed that frequent use of some cleaners, deodorants and aerosols appeared to increase the risk of diarrhoea, earache and other ailments in very young children, as well as headaches and depression in their mothers. Environmental campaigners believe potentially hazardous chemicals are also found in soap, hairspray, perfumes and cosmetics, and ironing boards and carpets.

Sunday Express, 24 October 2004

Enjoying the smell of a new car 'is like glue-sniffing'

The distinctive smell inside a new car, often a source of satisfaction to owners, comes from the same form of pollution that causes sick building syndrome, a study shows. New car smells could contain up to 35 times the health limit set for volatile organic chemicals in Japan, making its enjoyment akin to glue-sniffing. The chemicals found included ethyl benzene, xylene, formaldehyde and toluene used in paints and adhesives. Tim Williamson, of the National Society for Clean Air, said: 'So leaving the car at home is not only good for the environment, it is good for your health too.'

Daily Telegraph, 15 January 2003

COSMETICS AND NAPPY WIPES

Talcum alert after eight babies die

Eight babies have died through inhaling talcum powder during nappy changes, doctors said yesterday.

Daily Telegraph, 18 May 1991

Can cosmetics give children cancer?

Parents have been warned to keep their children away from cosmetics and toiletries because of fears that they may lead to infertility and cancer in later life. Parabens, which are routinely used in body lotions, can affect the female sex hormone oestrogen and were recently detected in breast cancer samples. Another study suggested pregnant women who rub creams into their skin to ward off stretch marks could affect the future fertility of their unborn baby boys. Parabens have been found in well-known brands of children's toilet wipes.

Daily Mail, 31 May 2004

Soap linked to childhood eczema, study

A huge rise in sales of soap products has triggered a sixfold increase in the number of children with eczema, according to research. Skin expert Dr Michael Cork found ... the spread of home comforts such as central heating and carpeting is also involved.

The consultant dermatologist urged parents to cut down on soapy detergents and baby wipes.

Daily Mail, 13 May 2002

THE DANGERS LURKING
IN YOUR HOME

Cancer in electric blankets

Cancer experts are planning the first nationwide investigation into links between electric blankets, home computers, pylons and childhood tumours.

Observer, 1990

Beware the killer lurking inside your shower

Shower curtains can be a breeding ground for deadly disease, say scientists. Billions of organisms can build up on a single vinyl curtain. Professor Norman Pace of the University of Colorado described the bacteria build up as 'soap scum'.

Daily Mail, 2004

Attack of the potting sheds

According to the Department of Trade and Industry's Consumer Safety Unit figures, there are 200,000 accidents in gardens every year. 'Hidden dangers lurk in the potting shed, with 2,000 gardeners injured by flower pots every year. Feet are impaled by forks, eyes are injured by flying twigs from edge trimmers, and ten people are electrocuted by their lawn mowers. Flower pots lead to bruised feet, broken toes and crushed fingers, while spades are responsible for 5,000 accidents a year.'

Daily Telegraph, 21 July 1994

Hidden risks of our hot houses

A hotter home can cause skin problems such as eczema, lethargy, poor concentration, disturbed sleep and fatigue. A rise in temperature of 7°F (4°C) could more than double bacterial growth rates, leading to higher risks of food poisoning and the spread of germs ... 'A hotter home can have an effect on your skin,' warned Dr Sarah Brewer, of the British Society for Allergy, Environmental and Nutritional Medicine.

Daily Mail, 23 October 2003

Halogen lamp poses cancer risk

Quartz halogen lamps, increasingly being installed at home and work, may put people at risk of skin cancer, researchers claim.

The Times, 10 April 1990

One in seven pools could be a danger to your health

Taking a dip is supposed to be good for your health. But bathers could be exposed to harmful bacteria every time they put a toe into the pool, a study has found … A separate study published recently found pregnant women who regularly take a dip in a swimming pool may be risking the health of their unborn child.

Daily Mail, 6 June 2002

Food mixers and vacuum cleaners linked to cancer

Common household appliances such as food mixers and hair dryers send out enough electromagnetic radiation to induce cancer, coronary disease, Parkinson's and Alzheimer's, according to a report leaked yesterday.

Irish Times, 10 April 1990

DRUGS

Anti-depressants 'link to risk of bleeding'

Patients taking anti-depressants may be more vulnerable to internal bleeding, doctors have warned. The risk of gastro-intestinal bleeding, which can have serious health consequences, is higher in patients who are also taking a daily aspirin or another non-steroidal anti-inflammatory drug.

Daily Mail, 9 March 2004

Aspirin study and risk of cancer

A study carried out on 88,000 nurses has found that those who took two or more aspirin a week for more than 20 years had a 58 per cent risk of pancreatic cancer. Those who took more than 14 tablets a week were 86 per cent more likely to develop the disease.

Sun, 23 October 2003

The dangers of HRT were overplayed, says expert

Hundreds of thousands of women who stopped taking HRT after safety fears would be better off going back on the drug, it was claimed yesterday. Up to a third of those who were taking the hormone replacement therapy stopped abruptly 18 months ago after an influential study warned it increased the risk of breast cancer, heart attack and stroke. But one of the doctors behind the study said that was the wrong choice for many struggling with menopausal symptoms. These women were now missing out on an effective treatment … The 'tiny' risk to health is outweighed by the benefits of the drug, according to Professor Susan Johnson.

Daily Mail, 16 February 2004

FOOD AND DRINK

Peril in bread roll: can hot dogs cause leukaemia?

Research has linked high consumption of hot dogs with an increase in childhood leukaemia.

The Times, 23 June 1994

Toast joins cancer danger list foods

Mushrooms, pepper, celery, coffee, potatoes and toast contain substances that can cause cancer, according to a study in the latest issue of the magazine *Science*. There are a large number of mutagens (gene-damaging substances) and carcinogens in every meal.

Scotsman, 17 September 1986

Scientists warn of toxins in fish

Each day at 4pm the trawlers come back, alive with giant bass, mackerel and squirming eels, at the end of a food chain that links family dinner tables to poisons in the sea. Besides mercury, which can damage the brains of foetuses and young children, and can affect healthy adults, there are PCBs, dioxins and flame retardants with unknown long-term effects.

Associated Press, 22 November 2004

Barbecued meat can be linked to cancer

Meat fried or barbecued for long periods and at high temperatures produces substances that have induced cancer in several species of animals, including monkeys, a scientist from the United States National Cancer Institute has reported.

www.forces.org

Why food fads can turn into a deadly obsession

An obsession with healthy food has led to the emergence of a new eating disorder. Sufferers become so concerned with eating only the healthiest and purest products that they avoid most foods found in supermarkets and end up starving themselves. One woman in the US is believed to have died from the condition, which doctors have labelled orthorexia, from the Greek word ortho, meaning straight and correct … An Italian study has suggested that the condition could affect as many as one in 14 people.

Daily Mail, 2 November 2004

Pickled food linked with throat cancer

Eating too many pickled onions increases the risk of throat cancer and a preference for taking very hot soup or drinks as well will increase the risk further.

Independent, 29 May 1992

Sex drive warning to vegetarians and elderly

Elderly and vegetarian men are being warned about the effect of low-protein diets on their sex lives in later years. Researchers say people who do not eat enough protein are at risk of low testosterone levels, which can cause a decline in sexual function as well as muscle loss, reduced red blood cells and damage to bones. People who do not eat meat are particularly at risk, because animal products are good sources of high biological value proteins.

BBC News Online, 21 January 2000

The dangers of herb tea

Herb Tea Linked with Liver Deaths.

The Times, 11 September 1992

Sushi may cut smokers' lung cancer risk, study suggests

Eating large amounts of sushi, the Japanese fish

delicacy now popular in many Western countries, may help smokers reduce the risk of developing lung cancer, scientists have said. Scientists at the Aichi Cancer Center in Nagoya, Japan, believe sushi and fresh fish are the reason lung cancer rates in Japan are markedly lower than those in the United States and Britain, even though the Japanese smoke as much as Westerners. 'Japanese people love their fresh fish, particularly sushi,' Professor Toshiro Takezaki said in a statement. 'We think that is why, even though the Japanese smoke as much as people in the UK, their rate of lung cancer is only two-thirds as high.' People who ate the most sushi and fresh fish had half the risk of developing the rare tumour than people who ate the least fresh fish.

Reuters, 3 May 2001

Soya 'risk' to unborn children

Pregnant women who eat soya could be endangering their babies, scientists warn. A chemical found in the bean plant may damage the sexual organs of boys in the womb and make them less fertile as adults, research shows.

Daily Mail, 13 February 2003

How soya could help men beat cancer

A diet rich in soy could protect men against prostate cancer, and even stop them going bald, according to research. A little-known molecule, created in the intestine when soy is digested, helps to 'block' a hormone that leads to prostate cancer.

Daily Mail, 14 April 2004

They hailed it as a wonderfood. But soya destroys forests and can be bad for your health

When we asked Dr Bill Helferich, a professor of food at the University of Illinois, what the implications were of increasing amounts of soya in the Western diet, he said: 'It's like roulette. We just don't know.' … The findings are inconclusive. Some case studies find soya reduces the risk of one cancer, but possibly increases the risk of another.

Observer Food Magazine, November 2004

Drinking milk 'raises cancer risk to women'

Drinking more than one glass of milk a day could double the risk of ovarian cancer, research has suggested. Researchers found that women who consumed a lot of dairy products were at significantly higher risk of serious ovarian cancer.

Daily Mail, 29 November 2004

Cereal linked to birth defects

Foods that are sugary or highly processed can as much as quadruple the risk of birth defects, according to research. Pregnant women who eat a lot of corn flakes, white bread, white rice or chocolate biscuits are putting their babies at risk of crippling abnormalities. Other dangerous foods include popcorn, chocolate bars, cooked carrots, honey and some soft drinks.

Daily Mail, 24 November 2003

Coffee and tea 'are as bad as cigs'

Tea, coffee, sugar and alcohol are 'social poison' as bad as cigarettes, a health group (Woman's Nutritional Advisory Service) claimed yesterday.

Sun, 25 March 1993

Chocolate every day keeps the doctor away

It makes you fat, it's loaded with caffeine, high in cholesterol, and bad for your skin. But chocoholics can take comfort from the good news that their guilt pleasure also has some health benefits. Hamburg–based DAK health insurance firm says eating chocolate actually cuts the risk of heart attacks. DAK says that the evidence is now strong enough that they have decided to encourage clients to eat more plain chocolate.

Deutsche Welle, 4 November 2004

We will have our peanuts back.

Canadian Airlines has cancelled a programme that offered peanut-free flights to passengers who suffer from a potentially deadly allergy. The programme was cancelled after 18 months when the airline realised it could not guarantee the safety of passengers prone to fatal peanut reaction, spokeswoman Diana Ward said. 'Our reviews indicated it was impossible to maintain a consistent level of service,' Ms Ward said. 'There just was no guarantee of a peanut-free environment. It was becoming unmanageable.'

Globe and Mail, 24 October 1996

Coffee linked with diabetes in babies

Pregnant women who are heavy coffee drinkers may be giving their unborn children diabetes, a study published today suggests. Researchers from Finland and America are pointing to a strong statistical correlation between countries with high coffee consumption and those with high levels of insulin-dependent diabetes, the type that usually affects young people.

Journal of the American Medical Association, October 1994

How a banana a day can keep strokes at bay

A daily banana is a good way of warding off strokes, scientists have found. An eight-year study of 5,000 men and women over 65 found those with the least potassium in their diet were 1.5 times more likely to have a stroke than those with the most. One large banana will contain around 500mg of potassium … Ripe bananas are also useful in the treatment of both constipation and diarrhoea.

Daily Mail, 13 August 2002

Why an apple a day won't keep the dentist away

An apple a day, so the saying goes, keeps the doctor away. But the dentist might disagree, after it was revealed that apples can be as bad for your teeth as sweets and fizzy drinks. Tom Sanders, a professor in nutrition and dietetics at King's College, London, studied tooth decay in youngsters and found that those from vegan or 'fruitarian' families, who eat only fruit, often had the worst teeth. Professor Sanders said: 'The research shows that snacking on fruit between meal is now bad advice.'

Daily Mail, 11 February 2002

Barbecues are the equivalent of 220,000 cigarettes

Barbecues should carry health warnings for releasing the same amount of toxic smoke as 220,000 cigarettes. Professor Desmond Hammerton, a retired biology professor from Callender, Scotland, said, 'Crowding round a barbecue throughout summer could have an effect on health over 10 or 20 years.'

Sun, 30 July 2003

How a salt-heavy diet can double cancer risk

A diet overloaded with salt is putting millions of us at twice the risk of contracting stomach cancer, research has revealed. Processed foods and ready meals are among the worst culprits but even everyday items such as bacon, bread and baked beans can boost salt to dangerous levels in the body. Eating just 12g of salt a day doubles the likelihood of stomach cancer, which kills more than 6,400 Britons a year, Cancer Research UK said yesterday.

Daily Mail, 7 January 2004

FOWLS

Pet birds blamed for lung cancer

People who keep birds are more likely to develop lung cancer, doctors in Holland have found. People who have kept birds at one time or another are seven times more likely to get lung cancer than people who have never kept birds … It may be that continuous bird keeping is as likely to cause lung cancer as continuous smoking.

Independent, 18 November 1988

INSOMNIA

Drugs legacy of poor childhood sleep

Children who sleep poorly are more than twice as likely to end up smoking, drinking and using drugs in their teenage years, scientists have found. A significant link between sleep problems in early childhood and 'risky' behaviour in adolescence was uncovered in a long-term study.

Daily Mail, 26 April 2004

LABELS

Lack of labels cause deaths

Up to 500 people a week are dying prematurely from heart attacks because the public is denied the nutrition information already required on pet food labels, health campaigners for the Coronary Prevention Group claimed yesterday ... deaths could be avoided if everyone used explicit packet warnings to help them tailor their diets to the lower fat and sugar guidelines by the Department of Health.

Guardian, 27 March 1992

Killer plants for sale at garden centres

The National Poison Unit called for all plants with poisonous leaves or berries to carry a skull and crossbones label. TV gardener Geoffrey Smith says, 'If it stops just one child being killed or hurt, it will have been justified.'

Sunday Express, 31 May 1992

MOBILES

Bad back risk from mobiles

The bad news for millions of addicts who see a stroll as an excuse for a gossip comes from Australian Dr

Paul Hodges, who studies spine disorders ... Apparently, if we talk at the same time, the breathing gets out of synch and the jolt registers on the spine. 'The spine is inherently unstable,' said Dr Hodges, 'and dependent on trunk muscles for stability ... We found the activity of the deepest abdominal muscle was reduced by 30-40 per cent during all speech tasks ... This compromise challenges spinal movement control, and may compromise spinal integrity.'

Daily Mail, 18 November 2003

OH ... ANYTHING REALLY.

Risk of being the first child

First-born children run a much higher risk of developing heart disease, according to a study. Scientists have discovered that eldest children could be up to 60 per cent more likely to suffer from Britain's biggest killer than younger siblings.

Daily Mail, 24 April 2002

SUN

Can the sun stop cancer?

Staying out of the sun could actually increase your chance of getting cancer, doctors are warning. They say lack of sunlight makes people more vulnerable to a range of cancers which kill more than 38,000 Britons a year … Vitamin D, the 'sun vitamin' which is produced by the body in response to solar exposure, has been shown to kill some tumours and stop others from growing in the first place. So staying in the shade can increase the risk of cancer, according to an expert at the University of California' Earlier this year Cancer Research UK launched its 'Sunsmart' campaign, which stressed the importance of staying out of the sun completely between 11am and 3pm, and always covering up with sunscreen, hats and T-shirts in the sun.

Daily Mail, 21 November 2003

TELEVISION

Insomnia link to excess TV watching

Children who spend hours in front of the television could be storing up sleep problems for later in life, say scientists … Dr Jeffrey Johnson, lead researcher, said: 'In the same way that teenagers should avoid cigarette smoking because it is associated with risk for a variety of health problems, heavy TV viewing, i.e. more than one to two hours per day, should be avoided.'

Daily Mail, 14 June 2004

VITAMINS

The vitamin boost that could cause early death

Thousands of Britons who take daily doses of vitamin E, one of the most popular dietary supplements, are risking premature death, research suggests. The latest study by scientists at John Hopkins University in Baltimore found that doses of 400 international units, often the equivalent of a single capsule, were associated with a 10 per cent increased risk of death.

The Times, 11 November 2004

WEIGHT

Fat drivers 'more at risk in crashes'

Overweight motorists are twice as likely as lighter people to be killed or seriously injured in road accidents, according to research. Those weighing between 15st 10lb and 18st 9lb were 2.5 times more likely to die in a crash than people weighing less that 9st 6lb.

Daily Telegraph, 6 August 2003

How 75% of Britons will be obese in just 15 years

Three out of four Britons could be overweight or obese within 15 years, health experts warned yesterday. And with the condition threatening to overtake smoking as the country's number one preventable killer, doctors are ill-prepared to deal with the problem, they added. A meeting of European obesity experts was told that many of today's overweight teenagers risk going blind or needing kidney transplants as a result of diabetes in their 30s ... An Obesity Task Force league table reveals that British women are the fattest in Europe while British men are the third fattest after Irish and Finnish men.

Daily Mail, 13 September 2002

NOW THAT'S MORE LIKE IT ...

Coke scare blamed on mass hysteria

The recent illness associated with Coca-Cola in Belgium may have been caused by fears over contamination rather than any impurities in the soft drink, members of the Belgian health council have said. Actual levels of contamination found in the soft drink were not high enough to cause the illnesses reported. Instead, anxiety following the recent dioxins scare and high media coverage of the issue may have caused people to react badly to small amounts of the smell of contamination not in the drink itself. 'The value of proposing this diagnosis is to recognise that victims, in this case the community, need social healing and not medical cure.'

BBC News Online: Health, 2 July 1999

AND IT WASN'T ALL BAD ...

Health experts say Stones hero Keith should have died eight years ago

He's notorious for his drug-taking, drinking, smoking and womanising but Rolling Stone Keith Richards' hell-raising antics may not have been as bad for him as people would expect. According to a leading expert on ageing, the 60-year-old guitarist should have died eight years ago [at the age of 52] due to his unhealthy lifestyle ... Mr Demko, who has served on two US governments [enquiries] into ageing, added: 'I'm not sure how he's done it but Keith Richards defies conventional wisdom.'

Daily Express, 25 February 2004

102 cheers old.

Widow Dorothy Peel toasted her 102nd birthday with half a pint of sherry, and put her long life down to a lifetime of fags and booze. Dorothy sinks the extra large measure of her favourite tipple every day, and that's just for BREAKFAST. She washes down lunch at her care home with a gin and tonic, and at bedtime she downs a whisky and dry ginger nightcap. But the boozy centenarian isn't all bad habits. Deciding she wanted to live longer she stopped smoking … when she was 99. Dot, of Bridlington, East Yorks, joked: 'I smoked for most of my life but packed it in three years ago. I smoked a packet a day and I still sneak a crafty one now and again…'

The People, 3 October 2004

THE DOs AND DON'Ts OF THE NEW POLITICALLY CORRECT SMOKING ETIQUETTE

DON'T offer your cigarettes round. They're too expensive

DO be courteous to non-smokers. Difficult we know but remember you're keeping up the good names of smokers

DON'T make a bonfire of the ashtray. Very unsociable, a fire risk and likely to set off smoke alarms. Embarrassing

DO avoid non-smoking homes. It will only cause irritation, bad tempers and irreparable damage to friendships

DON'T go to a hotel without first checking out the availability of smoking rooms

DO carry a receptacle in which you can place your fag ends. Life's tricky enough for smokers without being labelled litter-louts

DON'T get involved in rows about smokers' rights. You haven't got any

DO make sure when you smoke in a toilet you discard the evidence. A little bottle of air-spray helps. In dire straits squirt your breath freshener/perfume/aftershave

DON'T put a cigarette out in a waste bin. For God's sake do you want to get us all arrested

DO take your holidays in smoking countries. In Argentina and Cuba they allow smoking in some shops. Everybody, but everybody, smokes in China and civilised parts of Europe i.e. Spain and France

DON'T (we hate to insult your intelligence here) throw fag ends in a park, on dry land or bushes that look like a tinderbox. When a bush fire erupts it's only EVER a discarded cigarette to blame

CHAPTER THREE

SEX AND THE CIGGIE

WHY DO SMOKERS ALWAYS LOOK SO GODDAM SEXY?

Post-coital smoking passes the time while you wait for your cab

Three best things in the world: 'A drink before and a cigarette after.'

Anon

There are two kinds of smoking. Real smoking and sexy smoking. By this, we mean the difference between having a cigarette hanging seductively out the corner of your mouth, like Catherine Deneuve, who oozes sex appeal in the irritating way French women do when smoking, or looking like a Fagash Lil.

Put it this way, in *Monster* Charlize Theron puffed away like Trailer Trash woman. In the 1946 film *Gilda*, Rita Hayworth tossed back her long red hair, exhaled and she was christened a sex goddess. The cigarette did that for her. As it did for Marlene Dietrich, shrouded in thick clouds of billowy smoke in *Destry Rides Again*, and as cigarette-toting vamp Lola-Lola in *The Blue Angel*. Think James Dean in *Rebel Without a Cause*, posing with a ciggie in his petulant mouth, then look at Lee Marvin's cheroot in *Paint Your Wagon*. No comparison.

In the old days of black-and-white movies a cigarette was celluloid viagra. In the prurient decades

Marlene Dietrich enjoyed a fag, but never as much as everyone liked watching her smoke them.

before the Sixties, when cinema was a sex-free zone, Hollywood stars putting a cigarette between their lips and blowing was visual dynamite, the ultimate in sexual innuendo. The best, most memorable example of this was Bette Davis accepting one of the two cigarettes lit by Paul Henreid in the final scene of *Now, Voyager*, to the immortal line: 'Oh, Jerry, don't let's ask for the moon. We have the stars.' A scene that was reckoned to have pioneered the whole field of cigarette sex.

Back in the days BSWAS (Before Smoking Was A Swearword), an actor who knew how to use a cigarette was hot stuff; after winning a reputation as a sharp-tongued diva playing with menacingly long cigarette holders, Miss Dietrich got herself a lucrative advertising contract as poster girl for Lucky Strike cigarettes. She wasn't the only one laughing all the way to the bank. Film directors struck gold when they introduced the ciggie as a prop but it was never meant to be a weapon of mass seduction, more a solution to a problem that arrived with talking movies. What should actors do with their hands? Give them a cigarette, obviously.

As a sensual prop it was used to quite devastating effect. There's no doubt, the world's most proficient smokers were up there on the silver screen sharing post-coital cigarettes, anyone who sipped champagne, looked ravishing and smoked was obviously worldly enough to have sex.

And audiences loved it.

Those unable to afford mansion/yacht/fur coats/ diamonds or to be blessed with movie-star good looks could at least damn well share the dream with a smoke. A man with a cigar was associated with power. But women switched on to the idea that the act of smoking a cigarette, subtly choreographed to enhance their smouldering sexuality, could communicate their desire, or lack of it.

Quite useful really. Since a cigarette can be used as a prop for the coquettish 'come hither' look (model Kate Moss has this pose down to a fine art) or the provocative eff-off glare, it saves a lot of time in the chatting-up process. In fact, you can forgive a man for failing to discover the G-spot, but if he can't detect a woman's mood by the way she handles a cigarette he needs help.

Does she, for example, purse her lips as she smokes or pout between drags? When she stubs it out does she hurl it to the ground and ruthlessly stamp it to pulp on the pavement, or is she discreet? Does she blow delicate little smoke rings or evacuate her lungs with billowing clouds mid conversation? Does she caress the tip of her filter or merely suck it loudly?

Smoking involves more than lip eroticism. The diaphragm is involved too, causing the chest to swell and the stomach to contract. Put all this body language together and you've got a sexual barometer that's unbeatable. 'Smoking,' Catherine Deneuve says, 'is a visual and very attractive gesture, no?' Mais oui, Catherine. Just look at Anne Bancroft as husky-voiced Mrs Robinson, the full-on embodiment of corrupt and mature female sexuality in *The Graduate*. Using a cigarette as an erotic come-on, she says scornfully to Benjamin (Dustin Hoffman), 'Oh, yes. The track star doesn't smoke.' By the end of the movie he's a novice no longer. And he learns how to smoke too.

Once a boy has slept with an older woman, cigarettes obviously start getting a lot easier. Of course, until 1914 the concept of a woman smoking at all was alien and quite unacceptable unless you were a filthy rich 'It' girl or a member of the lower classes.

'Nice' girls smoked only at the risk of being labelled a slapper, tart or worse, debasing their status to that of someone a 'bit common'. Britain's Religious Tract Society informed young ladies that if they smoked they would become as low as 'this old Sally and that ancient Betty down in the dales or to the stalwart cohort of pit-brow women for whom sex has no aesthetic distinctions'.

Ooo-eeer, missus.

And, if that didn't put girls off, the Society also issued a helpful little warning that smoking would result in them growing moustaches as a result of 'constant movement of the lip'. Even with the acres of bad press cigs get these days and the appalling medical ailments that befall smokers, that was a new one on us.

In fact, it was a constant flexing of the muscles that truly brought about a change in attitudes towards women smoking. During the course of the war British women had been forced to take over jobs normally occupied by men, backbreaking physical work that, surprise, surprise, they were well able to handle. The munitions industry was reliant on a female workforce and by 1918, when factories wound down at the end of the war, women had begun to question the accepted notion that they should be doing servile jobs. Before 1914 they had happily followed their mothers and grandmothers down the well-worn path to domestic service. Now they had tasted financial independence, and the rituals of chastity and subservience no longer appealed as they wondered, quite rightly, why they should be serving tea, making beds and cleaning rooms for the idle rich.

In America of the 1920s, cosmopolitan women such as writer Dorothy Parker had taken to smoking as a badge of honour, and it wasn't long before the trend crossed the Atlantic and British women had pushed the consumption of tobacco to reach record levels. They were blazing a trail.

Women who smoked were suddenly deemed progressive and self-assured, not the common old Betty or Sally, but rather sophisticated. Meanwhile, the male association with cigarettes, cigars and pipes continued to be rooted in their macho ability to make decisions: the widely perceived view was that a man would use smoking to calm down, get a grip and take a wider view of the problem. Hence Humphrey Bogart's elevation from grumpy old git to machismo man in *The African Queen*, in which he chain-smoked throughout the entire movie. Nice work for a man who in real life was a prolific smoker.

Later generations would find their role models in rock and roll with Fifties stars Chuck Berry, Buddy Holly, Elvis Presley, Little Richard and Jerry Lee Lewis all smokers, all cool, all hip. But if anyone personified the tough-guy image of the smoker in

The light comes on again all over Europe ...

the Forties it had to be Bogie, America's most famous symbol of masculinity at the time. A smoker could get quite lyrical about the way he handles his cigarettes in *Casablanca*, taking smoking to an art form as he sticks his unfiltered in the corner of his lips, holds it between thumb and index finger, inhales big hits, blows smoke to the ceiling and nonchalantly flicks the ash to the floor.

FACT
The first line Lauren Bacall said to Humphrey Bogart in the film *To Have And Have Not* was 'Anybody got a match?' Bogart throws the matches at her. She catches them. They were put to good use, because the couple went on to light up 21 times in the film and got through two packs on screen. They later married in real life.

But even Bogie's legendary nicotine habit was overshadowed by that of James Bond, the first great post-war smoking hero. The idea of the world's most famous spy without a cigarette or a cigar would be about as likely as him telling a beautiful woman he was too tired for sex. 'He is the man every man wants to be and every woman wants between her sheets,' said the *Sunday Times* of 007, whose insatiable appetite for women was matched only by his passion for cigarettes: consuming sixty during a night in a casino was diddly-squat to 007, who would then move on to cigars.

By the time *Thunderball* came along, Bond author Ian Fleming conceded that all that smoke and copious amounts of drink might be taking their toll. So our hero was packed off to a health farm. Not to worry: a fortnight's abstinence, plenty of carrot juice, nut cutlets and steam baths had him back on top form and gasping for a fag.

FACT
Bond's preferred cigarettes were the imaginary 'Morland Specials'. They were made up to his own recipe of a blend of Virginian and Balkan weed by a bespoke tobacconist in St James's. He also smoked cigars while gambling in casinos. His boss M smoked a pipe. Sir Hugo Drax, the Moonraker villain, smoked a common brand of cigarettes. Well, he would, wouldn't he?

A PG-certificate has not yet been slapped on a film that contains a shot of someone smoking. But don't hold your breath.

Watch any old movie and you'll see the concierge, the doctor, the lawyer, his wife and her maid smoking. They were all at it, from the pimp to the parish priest who always had a pipe somewhere about his person.

In the film *Doctor In Clover*, actress Fenella Fielding even enjoys a post-operation puff in bed. The only place off limits in hospitals back then seemed to be the oxygen tent. Fair enough.

Nowadays, of course, smokers on screen are increasingly 'bad' people, prisoners, prostitutes, gunmen, gangsters, adulterers, bar-owners and alcoholics. Mass murderers usually, you'll find, enjoy a cigarette.

Smoking equals human vice.

Obviously, it suits the stressed-out emotional baddies. This development is hardly surprising, since over the past five years the pressure on the film industry to cut out the association between sex and the ciggie has been intense.

Yes, we know.

You must be totally astonished to learn that Hollywood has been asked to join the war on smoke by 'Smoke Free Movies' campaigners waving the catchy slogan: 'Tobacco-free film, Tobacco-free fashion'. Puritans have marched on Tinseltown in hob-nail boots begging film-makers to stub out

FACT
The extent of America's anti-smoking hysteria can be summed up in this piece of barmy research. Over to the Department of Statistics at the University of Guesswork. What do recent Hollywood movies *The Bourne Supremacy*, *I Robot* and *Spider-Man 2* have in common? Answer: They all have a 'sinister link'. They feature glamorous role models or villains smoking cigarettes. Apropos this fascinating discovery, researchers in New Hampshire have found that the more teenagers watch actors smoking the more likely they are to take up the habit themselves. Almost 5,000 children between the ages of nine and fifteen were surveyed. And guess what? Among those children who had been 'exposed' to more than 150 occurrences of smoking in a film, almost a third had tried cigarettes. Well fancy that!

Hollywood's fatal attraction with cigarettes. Evidently they have no objection to stars such as Catherine Zeta-Jones, Renée Zelwegger and Nicole Kidman lighting up the screen. But lighting up on screen? That makes them fume, though what possible threat Catherine Zeta-Jones poses to humanity by being pictured in *Chicago* with a cigarette is mystifying to say the least.

'Humphrey Bogart, Marilyn Monroe, Rita Hayworth and Cary Grant all looked sexier when smoking cigarettes because, contrary to what the doctors would have us believe, cigarette smoking is somehow rather sexy. Although the habit gave me up years ago, I miss it, especially when I go to the cinema. In the old days one could get through half a packet of fags during a good film. Now cinemas smell of popcorn and unpleasant exhalations.' Author A N Wilson calls on the British Medical Association to make films that contain smoking scenes PG-rated

Censoring history is probably not a good idea. As director Taylor Hackford points out: 'What we as directors should do is try to reflect reality. When we see films from the Forties, Fifties and Sixties, everyone is smoking. That reflects society's reality at that time. But for movies made in the new millennium, we should have less smoking because there is less smoking in society. But what the [social responsibility] task force are concerned with are attempts to rewrite history, having movies reflect the past with nobody smoking, or to insist that a film has no smoking even if smoking is part of the dramatic

'Here's lighting up for you, kid' Humphrey Bogart holds a flame for Lauren Bacall in *To Have And Have Not*

narrative the director is trying to create.' Of his movie *Ray*, a biography of Ray Charles, Hackford says, 'Anyone who knew Ray Charles, who was a smoker, would understand that if all of a sudden I had a smoke-free historical story of his life from 1935 to 1979, which is what my film covers, I'd be remiss and inaccurate. I feel it would be unconscionable for me not to present a real image.'

> **FACT**
> Most stars in the Forties and Fifties would have at least one still photograph in their publicity press packs of them smoking because it was deemed to be both sexy and glamorous.

Ah, but there's no pleasing some people. ASH even managed to be outraged when Gandalf was seen puffing a pipe in *Lord of the Rings* (does that mean he's got a bad hobbit?). Actually, it was the only reason some of us could think of for the movie winning so many Oscars.

How would these people have reacted in 1966 when Anne Bancroft (who appears to have cornered the 'Fagash Lil' market) appeared in *7 Women*? Smashing every latter-day taboo she plays a hardmoking doctor, holed up at a Christian mission under iege in China, who takes great delight in annoying he disapproving ladies running the place by having a cigarette constantly dangling from her lips. You get the lavour in the first scene when Bancroft comes down o dinner, takes a drag, stubs out her ciggie for grace, hen rekindles the embers and takes a deep drag, avouring it with her tongue, before exhaling coolly vith exaggerated pleasure. What a girl.

The point is this. Ever since Walter Raleigh hipped a boatload of tobacco to Britain, we've viewed smoking as something naughty but nice. Decadent but divine. A bit like sex, really.

OUR TOP TEN MOVIES THAT FEATURE SMOKING
Casablanca
To Have and Have Not
The Graduate
Now, Voyager
The Sweet Smell of Success
Body Heat
Blue in the Face
True Lies
The Blue Angel
Double Indemnity

Harry H Corb
steptoes into a sca
sexy new futu

THEY AD TO BE JOKING

SMOKING
IS GREAT
WITH LAGER

'The emphasis on the seductive evils of nicotine advertising seems to be over-stressed. I have worked in around 70 countries so far and some of the most nicotine-addicted nations I have ever come across were in countries which had no commercial advertising of any kind.'

Ann Leslie, journalist

There's an old saying: 'A cigarette is a pinch of baccy wrapped in paper with fire at one end and a fool at the other.' Quite unsaleable, you'd have thought. But James Buchanan Duke had a different view. In 1889 the founder of the American Tobacco Company recognised that, if dodgy elixirs and medicines that promised to cure everything from the common cold to gout could be shifted by advertising, then his cigarettes would walk off the shelves with a little judicious nudging and persuasion. The enlightened Mr Duke proceeded to spend $800,000 marketing his brand around the world, dreaming up advertising campaigns worthy of Saatchi and Saatchi along the way.

One inspired idea was to give smokers something for nothing, and so the idea of collectables was born in the form of cigarette cards. They were originally used to stiffen packets, but Duke turned them into a series of themed pictures. He was also responsible for cigarette posters, which, by the 1930s, were featuring doctors smoking with a cheery grin and dads dangling children on their knees while lighting up.

Either Duke was gifted with extraordinary foresight or just plain lucky, because advertising was to become, eventually, the epitome of modern culture. He depended on cheap newspapers, magazines, billboards and sandwich boards to sell his fags, but the 20th century would offer the unimagined opportunity of radio and cinema then, joy of joys, television: a personal cinema in your own front room.

This is when the cigarette advertisement came into its own.

In America, Lucky Strike jumped on the bandwagon by sponsoring a music show for teenagers called *Your Hit Parade*, which lasted seven years. Not to be outdone, in 1951 Philip Morris became sponsors of the comedy show *I Love Lucy*. It was a great move for star Lucille Ball: a demon smoker in real life, she was required to puff her way through vast numbers of cigarettes every week. In every respect Miss Ball was an ad man's dream. Successful, funny, famous, glamorous and a woman.

Since the end of the First World War and the

emancipation of women, consumption of cigarettes by the fairer sex had taken off to an extent that surprised tobacco manufacturers. Suddenly they were dancing, enjoying jazz, drinking and smoking. It crossed every social divide, mothers and daughters, marrieds and singles.

Both old and young now smoked openly. So how did advertisers propose to target women. The answer is as fascinating as it is hilarious.

So intense was the competition between rival tobacco companies to win over women that George Washington Hill, President of American Tobacco, called in Sigmund Freud's nephew, Edward Bernays, who involved himself in a variety of nefarious activities, such as placing news stories, organising press calls and funding balls, to demonstrate the cigarette as a symbol of the independent, free-thinking bold woman.

Public relations people and communications experts were brought to the table to discuss what sort of cigarette a woman really deserved. At one point it was referred to as a 'torch of freedom'. Maybe they were having a bad day. If focus groups had been invented back then, they would have been working flat out.

The long and short of it, advertising gurus

decided, was that the lady smoker wanted a brand she could call her own. A nictone-lite and feminine ciggie as opposed to the lung-busters blokes smoked. As pure as a mountain stream. Fresh-air clean. And it would be pretty. (We've heard cigarettes called many things, but pretty isn't one of them.) It would also, claimed manufacturers, keep a woman in shape for the new slim-line clothes designed for the sophisticated woman.

Hence Lucky Strike's famous slogan: 'Reach for a Lucky instead of a sweet.' The blatant selling of tobacco as a slimming aid was pounced on immediately, not by medics, but by US confectionery manufacturers who argued that tobacco was not a food and it was, therefore, fraudulent to claim a cigarette could be a substitute for a sweet. The company agreed to change the message to: 'Reach for a Lucky instead.' (Kylie Minogue really was born too late. Imagine the financial benefits of singing 'I should be so Lucky' in the Fifties.)

Meanwhile, Philip Morris brought out a new brand called Marlboro, which promised to be 'Mild as May'. A far cry indeed from the handsome, macho cowboy on horseback later christened 'Marlboro Man' and who would eventually be used to endorse the brand as something free of hazards, rugged and

Foiled by Moderation!
THE HEARTLESS SHADOW
that threatens the modern figure

"COMING EVENTS CAST
THEIR SHADOWS BEFORE"
(*Thomas Campbell, 1777-1844*)

AVOID THAT
FUTURE SHADOW

**by refraining from over-
indulgence, if you would
maintain the modern fig-
ure of fashion**

We do not represent that
smoking **Lucky Strike** Cigarettes will bring modern figures
or cause the reduction of flesh.
We do declare that when tempted to do yourself too well, if
you will "Reach for a **Lucky**"
instead, you will thus avoid
over-indulgence in things that
cause excess weight and, by
avoiding over-indulgence, maintain a modern, graceful form.

When Tempted
*Reach
for a*
LUCKY
instead

"It's toasted"

hearty, rather like the 'Marlboro Country' he came from. Originally, however, they were named (and abbreviated) after the Duke of Marlborough. The cigarettes were aimed specifically at 'decent, respectable women'. Marlboro were unique in that they provided an ivory tip of greaseproof paper to prevent them sticking to lipstick. 'That is why,' boasted Philip Morris, 'Marlboros now ride in so many limousines, attend so many bridge parties and repose in so many handbags.' Hmmm.

Inevitably some bright spark came up with the ultimate in nicotine nirvana. Combine the weed with chocolate. And so the 'cocoratte' was born, a 'soothing' blend of refreshing Colombian coco-leaf and 'the lightest Virginian tobacco' especially to satisfy a 'lady's need'. Sounds lovely. What more could a lady need than nicotine and chocolate? A dash of chardonnay, perhaps?

By 1967 the endless search was still on for the lady's perfect cigarette. American tobacco believed they had the answer in skinny, long Silva Thins, which made the staggering claim that 'Cigarettes are like girls, the best ones are rich and thin.' Er, perhaps not quite the message for the Swinging, anything-goes Sixties. More suited to the mood of the times was Philip Morris's slogan for rival brand Virginia

87

Slims: 'You've come a long way, baby.' And so too had the adverts.

Too far for the smoke police and politicians who began a campaign, lasting three decades, to purge the UK of 'glamorous' tobacco advertising. Two years after the advent of Virginia Slims, rumblings of dissatisfaction about cigarette advertising came to a head when the *Radio Times* implemented its own cigarette advertising ban. It was the beginning of a long and turbulent passage that would see all tobacco advertising – 'glamorous' had long since been replaced with 'any' – finally outlawed in the UK as of 14 February 2003.

One can only ponder Ann Leslie's words and consider the research that confirms that bans do not reduce smoking. In Russia, before 1989 when there were no adverts at all for cigarettes and no one was implored to visit Marlboro Country, smoking flourished. Is Britain a better place without the wit and wisdom of tobacco adverts? Certainly it is less colourful.

And possibly less safe. After all, would tobacco companies have developed filters and low-tar cigarettes had they been banned from advertising them?

We prefer to remember the days when smoking was not denigrated as a pursuit of the uncouth. They may be long gone, but in the world of advertising these examples of creative genius will never be forgotten.

'YOU'RE NEVER ALONE WITH A STRAND'

This belonged to the Fifties, the black-and-white era of TV and featured a Frank Sinatra lookalike, actor Terence Brooks, lighting up on a lonely street corner. The caption 'You're never alone with a Strand' proved to be one of the least successful of all time, since it implied that smokers were loners and Johnny no-mates who lurked beneath street lamps.

Needless to say, the ad went up in smoke and doubtless so did the career of the creative executive responsible for dreaming it up.

'I SMOKE 'EM BECAUSE MY NAME'S ON 'EM'

That was Reg, remember him? A rather stout chap who thought we'd like to try Regal because they were his brand of choice. The truth is that the tobacco industry did an about-turn and decided they would adopt the down-to-earth approach rather than the classy sophisticated image to sell cigarettes. It worked in that Reg became a national figure of fun. This was greeted by much tut-tutting from the advertising watchdogs, who claimed the introduction of a jocular character into the mean and moody world of tobacco advertising would only encourage youngsters to smoke. Er, no, we don't get the logic either.

Before the campaign was withdrawn, it was memorably parodied by *Viz* magazine with the caption: 'I smoke 'em because I'm clinically addicted to the nicotine.' Fair enough, smokers can take a joke. Non-smokers can't.

'CAN YOU GUESS WHAT IT IS YET?'

The Silk Cut adverts were probably the most literal of all tobacco adverts since the days when a beaming Ronald Reagan (yes, that's right, the former president of the USA once sold cigarettes) was pictured grinning inanely with a fag hanging from his lips and clutching a pack of Chesterfields. They featured a piece of purple silk with a bit snipped nearly out of it. And, er, that was it mainly. Eventually the 'cut' was not even shown, so implicit was the image. It ran for years and the final 'cut' for this advert came only when advertising in the UK was banned. But Silk Cut bowed out in style with a large woman dressed in purple silk apparently performing an aria. The caption: 'The fat lady sings'. Bravo.

'THEY'VE GONE DOWN.'
'NOT IN MY ESTIMATION, SIR.'

Lambert and Butler sound like a comedy act and the couple used to sell these cigarettes did succeed in making the public laugh. The jousting figures of rakish toff Lambert and his dour, unflappable Butler were on billboards all over Britain. They started off by exchanging wordplay related to the ever-decreasing price of the brand. 'They've gone down'

'But not in my estimation, Sir.'

'The price is frozen'

'Looks pretty hot to me, Sir.'

Their final appearance saw their faces blurred out like *Crimewatch UK* suspects while Butler mused: 'It seems we've been outlawed, Sir.' As kings of the billboards the couple managed to clock up eight years during the Nineties.

'READY RUBBED'

In the days when Dad sat down by the fire, slippers on and pipe in hand, the Christmas present problem was solved with a tin of St Bruno. To this day St Bernard dogs are still synonymous, to people of a certain age, with the tobacco the hound carried in its neck-mounted barrel. One can only wonder what lost explorers felt when they realised it wasn't

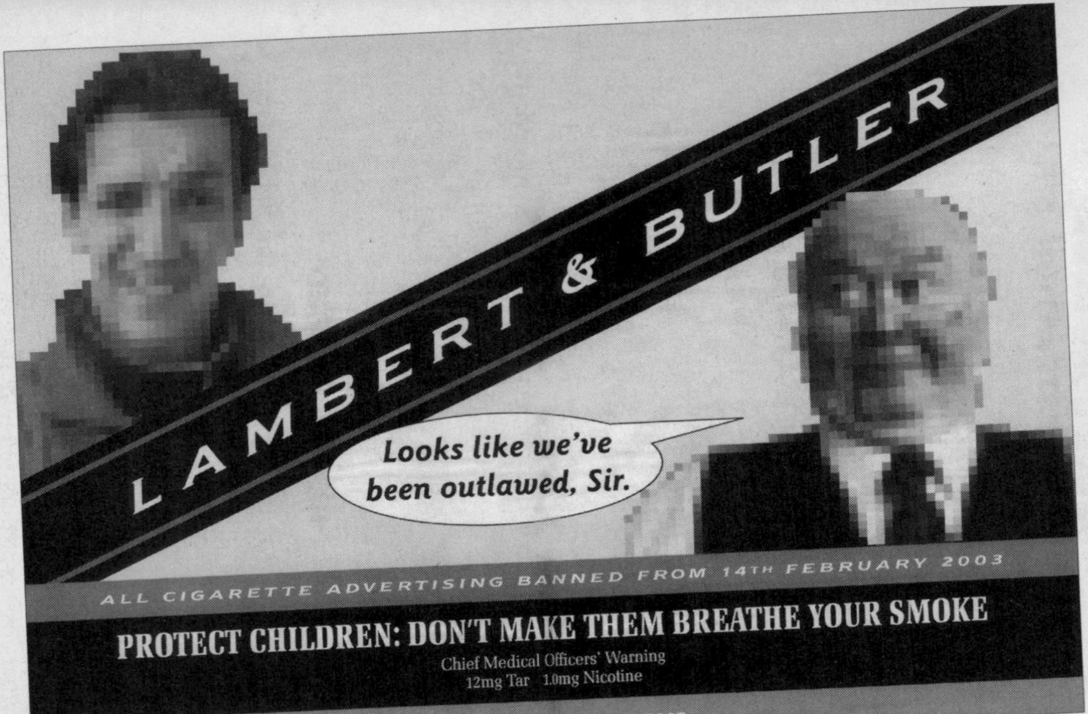

The Last Poster: February 2003

Happiness is a cigar called Hamlet.

Hamlet
MILD CIGARS

SMOKING CAUSES CANCER
Chief Medical Officers' Warning

brandy in that barrel, but several ounces of ready rubbed or flaked.

'HAPPINESS IS A CIGAR CALLED HAMLET'

Probably the most memorable tobacco advert of all time, the theme never changed from the central premise of promising troubled individuals, whether it was a sea captain whose crew deserted him when they spotted what they believed to be the edge of the world, or Morecambe and Wise haunted by Des O'Connor's singing, calm and relaxation with a cigar. All the adverts were accompanied by Jacques Loussier's rearrangement of 'Air on a G String' by Bach. Even now, go on, admit it, you still refer to that composition as the 'Hamlet tune'.

'COOL AS A MOUNTAIN STREAM'

An advert for Consulate, the menthol cigarette, was the second ever to be screened on British television and compared the invigorating, refreshing qualities of a mountain stream with tobacco. Ah, those were the days.

'MARLBORO COUNTRY'

Appealing unashamedly to men, the Marlboro Man

Come to where the flavor is.
Come to Marlboro Country.

Marlboro Red or Longhorn 100's you get a lot to like.

told us how things are in the wide, free Western plains of Marlboro Country. Constantly on horseback, the leather-clad cowboy conveyed the freedom of the traveller riding through rugged terrain, lassoing cattle and being generally macho. It's only fair to say that this hugely successful campaign backfired when two of the actors that had portrayed the Marlboro Man contracted lung cancer and became vehement anti-smoking campaigners.

'OPEN ALL HOURS'

Celebrities prepared to openly endorse tobacco were something of a rarity, so it's surprising, perhaps, that Ronnie Barker and David Jason were two prepared to trade their familiarity with TV audiences in a TV advertisement for Castella Classic cigars. In one sketch the pair were seen visiting a mate in prison and attempting to smuggle cigars in for him. It's since been debated whether, in fact, either actor actually smoked the Castella. On the other hand, we note that, when Steven Fry advertised for Panama cigars, he made smoking the product part of the deal.

FAMOUS PEOPLE WHO HAVE APPEARED IN TOBACCO ADVERTS

Marlene Dietrich
David Jason
Ronald Reagan
Eric Morecambe
Ernie Wise
Steven Fry
Gregor Fisher
Ronnie Barker
Penelope Keith
Rita Hayworth
Debbie Reynolds
Stefanie Powers

CHAPTER FIVE

SMOKE AND YOUR ARMS WILL FALL OFF, AND OTHER RIDICULOUS MEDICAL RESEARCH

Stopping smoking may reduce your breaks at work

For 500 years it seems that we have foolishly laboured under the misapprehension that smokers have reproduced like anyone else, and boasted some of the world's greatest lovers into the bargain. Ground-breaking research in this chapter now reveals the horrible truth. Smokers are a bunch of impotent, maladjusted inadequates, who can't sustain a marriage and cause cavities in little children.

Powerful gangs of men in white coats have long tapped in to the endless public-money fountain of 'research', and nothing inspires them more than the smoker, his sad life and above all his imminent rendezvous with death. Over the past decades, taxpayers of even the poorest countries around the world have unwittingly fed the cancer-scare machine with junk research showing that smokers are less virile, less intelligent, prone to hysteria, and more likely to go gaga and develop genital warts, though not necessarily in that order.

So under the shock-horror heading 'Teen Males who Smoke Risk Sperm Damage', we find a 'study' from the Livermore National Laboratory in the Czech Republic that claims young male smokers risk sperm damage that can cause genetic abnormalities in their children. Just 25 young men were enrolled in generating this unpleasant little research, yet its place on *News at Ten* is all but assured.

What about this little gem: 'Smoking May Increase Risk of Panic Attack'? (How the hell did that neurotic loser Churchill keep it together when faced with anti-smoking Hitler and his nerves of steel, and just which one shot himself in a bunker?)

Or this: 'Smoking Linked to Impaired Intellect', obviously referring to George Burns, who died aged 100 in possession of a razor-sharp mind after a lifetime of cigars and martinis, not to mention a well-publicised contempt for vegetables.

And finally, a triumphant piece of prize research from 'experts' at Harvard School of Public Health, which tells us that smoking kills 4.83 million (*exactly*) people worldwide every year. We would like to point out that this is the same school of health that threw up the 'experts' who claimed that men over 65 eating chocolate more than three times a month live a year less than those that don't, and that grandmothers who provide care to grandchildren for more than nine hours a week have a 55 per cent greater risk of heart attack. Oh well, we've all got to die some time. Here goes …

Non-smoking men have sex more often, and enjoy it more too

The Marlboro Man may look good in the saddle but he is likely not so good in bed, new research shows. Non-smoking men have more sex and enjoy it more than smokers, say scientists from the American Institute of Andrology in Lexington. It's unclear how cigarette smoking affects sexual behaviour and enjoyment. 'It is possible that smoking may act at different levels in the body, diminishing sexual frequency and satisfaction,' the researchers concluded.

National Post, 29 September 1999

Not only that but:

Smoking could reduce penis size

Smoking could reduce the size of a man's erect penis, researchers said. The shrinking manhood warning came from the Boston University School of Medicine when they revealed preliminary findings from a study of 200 men in the London *Observer* newspaper. Dr Pedram Salimpour said the findings were 'statistically significant' and promised to reveal them next month to the International Society of Impotence Research in Amsterdam.

Nando Times, 26 July 1998

Smoking late in life could impair intelligence in the elderly

A study by British and Spanish researchers found that those who smoked were four times more likely to show a decline in intelligence than non-smokers or former smokers. They said that their results show that smoking contributes to the clogging and hardening of the arteries and impairs the blood flow to the brain and other parts of the body. People who drank moderately were marginally less likely to have a decline in their mental powers than either heavy or non-drinkers, the researchers added.

Reuters (London), 18 April 2000

The effects of prenatal nicotine on human sexual orientation (or how smoking causes lesbianism.)

Prenatal nicotine exposure appears to significantly increase the probability of lesbianism among female offspring, especially if the exposure occurred in the first trimester along with prenatal stress in the second trimester. [Uh?] This study is the first to suggest that this drug has masculinizing/defeminizing effects on the sexual orientation of female offspring.

Minot State University, North Dakota,
29 October 2001

Smoking linked to genital wart duration

Genital warts are more likely to linger for six months or more in men who are smokers compared with non-smokers, according to a report presented at the First International Conference on Human Papillomavirus Infections [No, we don't know what that is either, but it sounds nasty]. In a study of 231 men being treated at the Perth STD Wart Clinic in Australia, men with visible warts were younger and nearly three times more likely to be current smokers than men without warts, reported Dr Jenny McCloskey. Patients who had warts that lingered for six months or longer were twice as likely to be smokers. Men who had warts for 31 months or longer were more than six times more likely to be smokers than non-smokers. The findings are 'biologically plausible', McCloskey noted.

Reuters, 13 July 1998

Second-hand smoke may cause cavities in children

Children whose parents smoke are more likely to develop dental cavities according to a study from the University of Rochester's Strong Children's Research Center. 'This study should serve as a sobering wake-up call to parents who still don't see the danger in smoking around their children,' says paediatrician Andrew Aligne. 'We already know smoking isn't good for us and here's another reason. New research shows that second-hand smoke may cause cavities. Maybe that's another reason you should try to quit.'

University of Rochester Medical Center,
30 April 2001

Breast cancer link to smoking at puberty

Girls who smoke, or are exposed to passive smoking, around the time of puberty may be at considerably increased risk of developing breast cancer in later life, said Robert Burton, Director of Anti-Cancer Council of Victoria. But his proposition has been strongly rejected by leading breast cancer specialists, who argue that it is not backed by sufficient research and flies in the face of other observations of the disease.

Australian, 24 November 1999

Teen males who smoke risk sperm damage: study links birth defects to tobacco

Teenage males who smoke cigarettes appear to be risking sperm damage that can cause genetic abnormalities in their children, researchers said yesterday. Although the smoking portion of the study enrolled only 25 young men for detailed analysis, the results were enough to trigger new warnings about the potential hazards of cigarettes, especially among young men who also drink alcohol.

San Francisco Chronicle, 2 October 1998

Smoking during pregnancy linked to mental illness

Women who continue to smoke after they know they are pregnant may be more likely to be mentally ill than non-smoking women, according to new preliminary findings. Dr Louise H Flick of St Louis University said that, 'Women in our low-income sample who continued to smoke after they knew they were pregnant were almost five times more likely to have a current psychiatric illness than were women who had not smoked in the last year.'

Reuters, 22 October 2001

Smoking mums recipe for tantrums

Children whose mothers smoked during early pregnancy are more likely to be aggressive and display delinquent behaviour then they grow up. Dr Richard Roylance, a consultant paediatrician to Queensland Health, said the research was another 'nail in the coffin' for companies who 'allegedly' targeted young women as smokers.

Courier-Mail, Brisbane, 8 January 1999

BUT SOMETIMES THE RESEARCH WENT OUR WAY ...

Warning: nicotine seriously improves health

Nicotine, the drug that has addicted millions to the smoking of cigarettes, could soon be rehabilitated, as a treatment for schizophrenia, Alzheimer's and Parkinson's diseases, and hyperactivity disorders. Research has shown the chemical has a powerful impact on brain activity in patients suffering from psychiatric and degenerative disorders.

Observer, 18 July 2004

Passive smoking doesn't cause cancer – official

The world's leading health organisation has withheld from publication a study which shows that not only might there be no link between passive smoking and lung cancer but that it could even have a protective effect. The astounding results are set to throw wide open the debate on passive smoking health risks ... and are certain to be an embarrassment to the WHO, which has spent years and vast sums on anti-smoking and anti-tobacco

107

campaigns. The study is one of the largest ever to look at the link between passive smoking and lung cancer, and had been eagerly awaited by medical experts and campaigning groups.

Sunday Telegraph, 8 March 1998

Ten a day OK, smokers told

One of Britain's top experts on the effects of smoking has provoked outrage in the anti-cancer establishment by insisting it's fine to smoke 10 cigarettes a day, passive smoking is no problem, and the government is wasting money telling people to quit. Dr Ken Denson of the Thame Thrombosis and Haemostasis Research Foundation in Oxford has spent the last decade studying smoking-related illnesses and concluded that the real problem isn't the cigarettes, but the poor diet of smokers. 'Smokers with the right diet can have an 80% lower risk of cancer than the smoker on a bad diet,' said Denson, claiming that both smokers and drinkers are being deliberately misled on their habits' risk levels.

Three Cheers for Ken Denson. Hip Hip …

CHAPTER SIX

A WRITE-ON PROFESSION: THE ROLE OF CIGARETTES IN BOOKS AND JOURNALISM

'When on occasion I'm asked by groups of aspiring writers what they should do to get on, my advice is always, emphatically, smoke. Smoke often and smoke with gusto. It's a little known, indeed little researched, fact of literature and journalism that no non-smoker is worth reading. And writers who give up become crashing bores.'

A A Gill, Sunday Times, July 1999

Journalism is a hazardous occupation

All those wars and disasters. Then there's the smoking and drinking. Meat and drink before BSWAS (Before Smoking Was A Swearword). I arrived in Fleet Street three decades ago when newsrooms looked like a cross between Saturday night in an A&E ward and a war zone. Offices were nicotine brown and ceilings gunge-covered. Waste bins regularly went up in flames as fag ends smouldered alongside discarded stories. You could flick ash over the old stand-up Remington and it would fall straight through; try that with a computer and expect it to function. I'll be honest, floors were ashtrays. Writers would go missing in the clouds of billowing smoke that followed them from desk to pub where, with a pre-prandial drink before a robust lunch, they'd demolish a pack of twenty.

Like ace reporter Hildy Johnson in the seminal

newspaper movie *His Girl Friday*, the idea of a journalist hitting the keyboard of a clapped-out old typewriter without a fag would have been preposterous, rather like Posh without Becks, cheese without pickle or Benson without Hedges.

'Cigarette me,' yells Hildy as she hammers out a world-beating exclusive. Now, of course, that bit would end up on the cutting-room floor, censored by the smoke police. Anyway it's hardly a scenario you're likely to encounter in any of the great newsrooms these days, places which resemble insurance offices or strictly no-smoking, spookily silent, New Age centres.

No one, of course, has ever been able to prove, conclusively, that working in a homogenous, sterile environment is better for the creative juices than sitting in a bar room with a gang of hacks puffing Camels. Except, of course, that history has delivered us thousands of authors, playwrights and journalists who thrived on tobacco, worshipped it, even.

'The harder I work,' wrote *Whisky Galore* author Compton Mackenzie, an inveterate and determined smoker who lived to the grand age of 89, 'the more I need to smoke because tobacco is the handmaiden to literature.' He was 74 when he wrote his 81st book, *Sublime Tobacco*, the point of which was to prove his theory that smoking is 'one of the greatest boons ever conferred upon humanity'.

Something journalist-turned-playwright Dennis Potter agreed with. Identifying the writer's need for the adrenalin to be found in a cigarette he summed it up perfectly. 'Nobody has yet been able to demonstrate to me,' he told the *Sunday Times*, 'how I can join words into a whole sentence on a blank page without a cigarette burning away between my lips.'

He spoke for the frantic, wild-eyed reporter, columnist or feature writer, with a fag stuck in the corner of their mouth, working towards a deadline. Author Martin Amis admits that without a cigarette he fears what might happen to his writing skills. 'I might end up writing lines like: "It was bitterly cold" or "It was baking hot,"' he told *The Paris Review*.

Heaven forbid.

Lord Byron would never have contemplated picking up a pen without a smoke. 'Sublime Tobacco.' he wrote. 'Which from East to West/Cheers the tar's labour or the Turkman's rest/Yet thy true lovers more admire by far/Thy naked beauties, Give me a cigar.' William Makepeace Thackeray, Coleridge and Lord Tennyson, who would only visit the Prime Minister Gladstone, if he was given a bedroom in which he could smoke his pipe, all believed that smoking spurred them on.

Perhaps Anthony Trollope really hit the nail on the head with the view that, 'It has been the companionship of smoking that I have loved, rather than the habit.' Writing is a lonely occupation which requires peace and clear thinking and, while drinking, as Mark Twain explained, 'clogs the brain', he found as so many journalists and authors do 'smoking to be the best of all inspirations for the pen'. Three hundred cigars a month, he reckoned, was a 'sufficient amount to keep my constitution on a firm basis'. All well and good, but one has to wonder what it did to his bank balance.

Meanwhile, back in 1882 Professor Thomas Edison had already decided there was nothing to perk up the old grey matter like an ounce of baccy: 'I think,' he wrote, 'chewing tobacco acts as a good stimulant upon anyone engaged in laborious brain work.'

How true. One of your authors, Sue C, draws the line at chewing tobacco herself, but has, in the process of writing this book, probably managed to puff her way through 5,000 cigarettes. A minuscule drop in the ocean to the number she's consumed since, at 19, she had her first drag: a menthol, what a wuss, but it was the gateway to hard-core nicotine. The sort Fleet

Street preferred. It was wildly optimistic, of course, for smokers like Sue C to presume that newspaper offices like any other would continue to be the nicotine nirvanas of the modern world:

'Around the early Nineties, it dawned on newspaper proprietors that their hugely expensive premises were in danger of going up in smoke. Also, being caring and (ahem) compassionate employers, they developed previously well-concealed concerns about the health of the workforce. This was a nonsense, it merely suited them to have cleaner offices and a suppressed staff. If they could control the smoking, a purge on alcohol would surely follow. Which it did.

'I worked at the *Sun* newspaper during those heady days when a 'smoking ban' seemed as ludicrously unlikely as New Labour winning the general election. Hah. The first referendum asking journalists if they would prefer a smoke-free office was conducted, with all the pious evangelism of a former sixty-a-day man, by editor Kelvin MacKenzie in 1990 and was a complete failure, largely because I took it upon myself to photocopy the ballot papers causing electoral chaos and a huge 'No' to the ban. I also bribed colleagues, having never met a hack who couldn't be corrupted by the offer of a restaurant bill to supplement expenses or a free drink.

'The smoking fraternity actually believed that was it. End of story. We had slayed the monster and would be left alone to enjoy our cigarettes in peace and continue writing our stories enveloped in that familiar, comforting fog of smoke. It was a feeling of exhilaration we were fated not to experience again, though, as the fresh-air Nazis closed in on the world of journalism and publishing.'

Of course, we now realise this was just a microcosm of what was going on all over Britain at the time. For every *Sun* newsroom there was a Halifax Building Society imposing their own bans and denigrating smokers antisocial, uncouth and evil.

Happily, there is little the anti-smoking brigade can do thus far to censor – though don't hold your breath – anyone writing about the cigarette, the cigar or the pipe. Or, indeed, the delirious pleasure of smoking.

And thank God for that.

As an aid to characterisation, the novelist would be lost without a cigarette. In fact, literature might be scattered with unsolved crimes had the fictional detective been deprived of nicotine. Sherlock Holmes without his pipe?

Actually, crime genius or not, he came dangerously close to being a tobacco bore: 'I have as you know,' he relates in 'The Boscombe Valley Mystery' (in Arthur Conan Doyle's *The Adventures of Sherlock Holmes*) after identifying ash as coming from an Indian cigar, 'devoted some attention to this, and written a little monograph to the ashes of 140 different varieties of pipe, cigar, and cigarette tobacco.' Yawn.

Or how about Mickey Spillane's detective Mike Hammer minus the ubiquitous Lucky Strike? In his novel *Lady in the Lake* Raymond Chandler observed: 'Three hundred yards from the gate a narrow track, sifted over with brown oak leaves from last autumn, curved around a granite boulder and disappeared. I followed it around and bumped along the stones of the outcrop for fifty or sixty feet, then swung the car around a tree and set it pointing back the way it had come. I cut the lights and switched off the motor and sat there waiting. Half an hour passed. Without tobacco it seemed a long time.'

Other fictional detectives who smoke include Maigret, Inspector Dalziel, Columbo and Philip Marlowe. And, obviously, it makes sense that the author who smokes would be most inclined to bestow the habit on their creation. For example, P G Wodehouse, who believed that if authors failed to smoke in photographs they deprived the public of knowing whether or not they were 'manly', recognised that when Jeeves faced a domestic crisis, such as what tie to wear, only a cigarette would do the trick.

Oscar Wilde was a man with an enormous appetite for tobacco, so it's little wonder that, in *A Picture Of Dorian Gray*, Dorian announces: 'Will you have some coffee, you fellows? Waiter, bring coffee, and fine champagne, and some cigarettes. No: don't mind the cigarettes; I have some. Basil, I can't allow you to smoke cigars. You must have cigarettes. A cigarette is the perfect type of a perfect pleasure. It is exquisite, and leaves one unsatisfied. What more can one want?'

And only a former twenty-a-day woman like Helen Fielding could write with such compassion about the misery facing the young, single girl in today's anti-smoking climate. In *Bridget Jones's Diary* her heroine recalls a train journey: 'Ugh. "Smoking Carriage" turned out to be Monstrous Pigsty where smokers were huddled, miserable and defiant. Realise it is no longer possible for smokers to live in dignity, instead being forced to sulk in slimy underbelly of existence. Would not have been in the least surprised if carriage had been shunted off into siding never to be seen again. Maybe privatized firms will start running Smoking Trains and villagers will shake their fists and throw stones at them as they

117

pass, terrifying their children with tales of fire-breathing freaks within.'

Girls and smoking in literature are not exactly, however, a new phenomenon. Way back in 1880, Emile Zola wrote admiringly of the courtesan Nana (in his book of the same name) that she 'kept rolling cigarettes, rocking backwards and forwards on her chair as she smoked them'. It was her love of tobacco, undoubtedly, that enhanced Nana's sexual allure, whereas years later, in Evelyn Waugh's *Vile Bodies*, 'Agatha Runcible brandishes a cigar to portray her irreverence for everything, men, money, society, politics, the lot. She smokes Turkish cigarettes with vigour, ignores No Smoking signs and is disdainful of serious matters like politics.'

But the last word in cigarettes and literature must go to Anthony Burgess's immortal opening words in *Earthly Powers*: 'It was the afternoon of my eighty-first birthday, and I was in bed with my catamite when Ali announced the Archbishop had come to see me. I lay a little while, naked, mottled, sallow, emaciated, smoking a cigarette that should have been postcoital but was not … a Fribourg and Treyer cigarette in its Dunhill holder relating me to an era when smoking has been an act to be performed with elegance.'

I'll raise my B&H to that.

WRITERS ON SMOKING
IN THEIR OWN WORDS

'The happiest sight in the world … a black coffee, a computer and a pack of twenty.'

Bruce Robinson, author of *Withnail & I*

'Bereft of the weed owing to the anxiety of my nearest and dearest, and aware that I am lucky to have reached the age at which it used to be normal to die, I can only say that ciggies were lovely and that maybe, when I reach the end, I shall be allowed a last "magical" inhalation.'

Beryl Bainbridge

'Day by day in every way we smokers are being harder pressed. Like the troops of Midian, the enemy prowl around. First it was James the Second [sic], then Tolstoy, then all these doctors, and now, of all people, Miss Gloria Swanson, the idol of the silent screen, who has not only become a non-smoker herself but claims to have converted a San Franciscan business man, a Massachusetts dress designer, a lady explorer, a television script-writer and Chicago dentist. "The joys of not smoking," she says, "are so much greater than the joys of smoking", omitting, however, to mention what the former are. From the fact that she states that her disciples send her flowers, I should imagine she belongs to the school of thought which holds that abstention from tobacco heightens the sense of smell. I don't want my sense of smell heightened. When I lived in New York, I often found myself wishing that I didn't smell the place as well as I did.'

P G Wodehouse

'When I was young and very poor … I determined that if I ever had any money I would smoke a cigar, every day after luncheon and after dinner.'

Somerset Maugham

'A great development from the persecution [of smokers] has been the spirit of solidarity which has arisen among smokers. Long may it prosper, if we are prepared to abandon our freedom of choice in this matter, we might as well accept direction on what we eat, drink, wear, say and think.'

Auberon Waugh

'I do not believe that intelligence and creative thinking are injured by smoking.'

Emile Zola

When Raleigh, in honour of whom England should have changed its name, introduced tobacco into this country, the glorious Elizabethan age began. I am aware that those hateful persons called Original researchers now maintain that Raleigh was not the man, but to them I turn a deaf ear. I know, I feel, that with the introduction of tobacco England woke up from a long sleep. Suddenly a new zest had been given to life. The glory of existence became a thing so to speak of men who had hitherto only concerned themselves with the narrow things of home, put a pipe into their mouths and became philosophers. Poets and dramatists smoked until all ignoble ideas were driven from them, and into their place rushed such high thoughts as the world had not known before. Petty jealousies no longer had hold of statesmen, who smoked and agreed to work together for the public weal. Soldiers and sailors felt when engaged with a foreign foe, that they were fighting for their pipes. The whole country was stirred by the ambition to live up to tobacco. Everyone, in short, had now a lofty ideal constantly before him.'

Sir John M Barrie

'I would argue that every man, whatever his race
whatever his rank, whatever his profession, whateve
his work, is helped by smoking.'

Sir Compton Mackenzi

'There's a whole generation of puritans growing u
which I can't bear the thought of. Thank God
won't be here to put up with them in twenty year
time. The next thing is these anti-smoking peopl
will move on, inevitably, to drinking and people wil
start talking absolute crap about passive drunks.
know drunks are a bore but at least smokers aren't.'

Jeffrey Bernar

'What is this smoking that it should be considered
crime? I believe in my heart that women are jealou
of it, as a rival, They speak of it as of some secret
awful vice that seizes upon man, and makes him
Pariah from genteel society. I would lay a guinea tha
many a lady who has been kind enough to read th
above lines, lays down the book after this confessio
of mine and says, "Oh, the vulgar wretch." and passe
on to something else.

'The fact is, that the cigar *is* a rival to the ladie
and their conqueror, too.'

William Makepeace Thackera

'The man who smokes thinks like a sage and acts like
a Samaritan.'

Edward Bulwer-Lytton

'May my last breath
be drawn through a pipe
and exhaled in a jest.'

Charles Lamb

Only a fool expects smoking and drinking to bring
happiness, just as only a dolt expects money to do
so. Like money, booze and fags *are* happiness and
people cannot be expected to pursue happiness in
moderation. This distillation of ancient wisdom
requires constant reassertion as the bores and
prohibitionists and workhouse masters close in.'

Christopher Hitchens

In these days of spasmodic speed, volcanic rush, and
eternal hurry, when quiet has lost its meaning and
speed, not perfection, is the universal aim, tobacco
affords a man a resting-place and shelter from
storm and stress. Smoking leads to contemplation
and meditation. There are people who cannot do
nothing: inaction is impossible to them, and yet
though eternally busy they do nothing. A smoking

123

man may be slow to commence, but he accomplishes his task better than the fraternity of fuss.'

W A Penn, *The Souverane Herbe: A History of Tobacco*

CHAPTER SEVEN

I DON'T BELIEVE IT! THE CRAZY, THE BANAL AND THE DOWNRIGHT DISGRACEFUL

Get laid
start
smoking:
It looks
cool

SOME OFF-THE-WALL STORIES
DEVOTED TO THE WEED

The first menthol cigarette to be introduced went under the unlikely brand name 'Spud'. Yeah, before you ask, for spud read 'dud'. It was swiftly overtaken by the fresher, mintier-sounding 'Kool'.

In the First World War, the *People* newspaper called on its readers to send Woodbines, Tommy's favourite fag, to the Western Front. They could buy them at ten for a penny, or contribute to their massively oversubscribed 'Tobacco Fund'. Would anyone be so quick to send ciggies to Iraq, we wonder?

When rock 'n' roller Jerry Lee Lewis lit up his cigarette on stage in 1958 he also set fire to his piano. He proceeded to pour petrol on it with one hand, while banging out 'Whole Lot of Shakin' Going On' with the other.

Triumph International (Japan) Ltd has announced the new must-have underwear: a fragranced bra that, it claims, will help women smokers to give up. A tiny, hidden capsule sited near the cleavage will release fragrances such as lavender and jasmine, smells its makers say will lower the wearer's desire for a cigarette. They say that the new bra is unlikely ever to be sold in shops. We can't think why.

Author John Braine was way ahead of his time by inventing the cigarette sticker for his own entertainment two decades ago. The heavy smoker would attach the words 'Cigarettes are Good for You, Smoke More, Live Longer' to his pack when going out for a drink.

The first chewing tobacco was called 'Fudgeon' and was popular with sailors. Schoolboys, emulating cowboys chewing tobacco, discovered early in life (and without the intervention of finger-waggers) that the habit wasn't just revolting, it made you heave. All day.

A controversial new fatwa has been issued in Egypt, ruling that having a smoking spouse is legitimate grounds for divorce. The ruling was made by the country's mufti Farid Naser Wasel, at the request of an anti-smoking campaign group after a fatwa against cigarettes was ignored. It is rumoured that the institution of marriage could go up in smoke.

127

The longest cigarette holder in a film was held by Harpo Marx in *A Night in Casablanca*.

Michael Todd Jnr was the innovator who made a 'smellie' movie called *Scent of Mystery* in 1960. The Technicolor thriller was made in Smell-o-Vision in 1960 and scents included ocean oxone, garlic, oil paint, wine, boot polish and pipe tobacco. They were piped to each cinema seat on cue from the 'smell-track' of the film. Nice idea but the movie, apparently, was a stinker.

The people of Springfield (no, not that one) were told they could sleep more easily in their beds knowing they had been saved from a tobacco-crazed fireman. John S Marrero was driving erratically and was found to be in possession of crack cocaine when he was stopped by a state trooper but it was the fact that he was smoking a ciggie that clinched his dismissal. He was the first in the state to be fired under a law prohibiting fire fighters and police officers from smoking on or *off* duty.

The first official smoke haters were the British Anti-tobacco Society. It was formed in April 1853 and consisted of assorted scientists and crusading evangelicals. No change there, then.

A supervisor at a firm with a strict no-smoking policy was sacked for allegedly lighting a cigarette in his car as he left at the end of a night shift. A video camera at the factory, which supplies printed wrapping materials to the tobacco industry, recorded a flash of light in the car. Employers studying CCTV film for evidence of smoking violations? Surely the ghetto cannot be far off ...

The first man to make smoking magic was English performer Richard Pitchford, born in 1899. The magician took to the stage in white tie, tails, white gloves and top hat , then, pretending to be drunk, he attempted to steady his hand before fitting a cigarette holder between his teeth. The ciggie kept disappearing and reappearing. He finally lit it with a match that fell into his hand. Lighted cigarettes began plaguing him one after the other, till finally he landed a lighted cigar. When he walked off stage a large, lighted pipe appeared from nowhere. He smoked it, naturally.

Smokers are more prone to divorce, according to a new survey conducted by the University of Chicago. 'This research that found smoking rates were far above average in women and men who later divorced is saying something really new and different,' said researcher Eric Doherty. Congratulations, Eric, that's really worthwhile work, now perhaps you could do something useful and find a cure for cancer.

Former owner of the *Daily Mirror* Robert Maxwell so disliked smoking in the office that he reprimanded a man smoking as he was getting into the lift at the newspaper. He demanded how much the man earned a week and the offender replied, 'Seventy-five pounds.' Pulling out a fat wallet, Maxwell reeled out three hundred pounds, which covered a month's wages, handed it to the smoker and said, 'You're fired.' Little did he know, the man was not an employee but a visitor. He later regaled *Mirror* staff with the story of the best day's money he'd ever earned.

POWs in the real-life Great Escape of 1944 were encouraged to smoke as many pipes and cigarettes as possible in the camp theatre to disguise the smell of the tunnel sand hidden under the seats.

In a 1962 comedy sketch, Bob Newhart played an Englishman getting a phone call from Sir Walter Raleigh in America: 'Don't tell me, Walt, don't tell me, you stick it in your ear, right Walt? Oh, between your lips. Then what do you do to it? (Giggling) You set fire to it. Then what do you do, Walt? You inhale the smoke. … Walt, we've been a little worried about you … you're gonna have a tough time getting people to stick burning leaves in their mouth …'

In November 2004, the *New York Post* ran a front page of a US Marine in battered helmet, face streaked with sweat, nose gashed, eyes narrowed, smoking a cigarette after a skirmish in Fallujah, Iraq. The response from the readers was astonishing. Far from praising soldiers and showing gratitude, the majority protested about the cigarette. 'How much did Philip Morris pay you for the advertisement?' asked one, while another bleated, 'Thank you for continuing to encourage the development of cancer.' Clearly, it's safer to light up in Fallujah than in Manhattan.

From the *Philadelphia Inquirer*, 28 April 1996: 'In Boulder, CO, USA, smoking has been banned in all public buildings including the Boulder Dinner Theater. The ban hit trouble when they put on a production of the Broadway musical *Grand Hotel*, which includes a one-minute scene where a couple of characters smoke. After an outraged theater-goer called the police, the owner of the theater was ordered to cut the scene or face 90 days in jail and a $1,000 fine. Trouble was, copyright law forbids him to alter the scene at risk of civil litigation. "It's so funny," said the copyright owner of the play. "In these censorious times, everyone goes home and sits around the dinner table and talks about how great it is to live in a free country.'" Quite. We couldn't have put it better ourselves.

From ASH USA comes the news that smokers murder more people in the workplace than, well, murderers. 'Workers are much more likely to be killed by smoking co-workers than by robbers or disgruntled employees,' says John Banzhaf, Executive Director of ASH.

In the hit Sixties TV series *Dr Kildare*, the handsome medic played by actor Richard Chamberlain was seen in the first ever scene buying cigarettes from a machine in the hospital. He frequently offered a light or a cigarette to his patients.

Brian Morrison was fired up to be a Boca police officer, but his chances went up in cigar smoke when he learned that a few puffs on a stogie to celebrate his college graduation violated the city's rule banning tobacco use by police officers. 'I had a cigar at my graduation and at a friend's birthday party,' said Morrison, who admitted his tobacco use during a polygraph test. 'I didn't think it counted.' Job applicants must sign an affidavit swearing they have not used tobacco in the past year and agree not to start if they are hired. 'Obviously if you're a regular smoker, you're out,' said the city's employee relations director Bill Katz, adding, 'When that mugger has got a knife to your throat the last thing you need is a policeman who smokes.'

OK, we made that last bit up, but you get the picture.

A fugitive Mafia convict gave his hideout away after police spotted his pile of cigarette butts outside his window. Police said Votano, 30, gave himself away by throwing hundreds of cigarette ends from a tiny window of his lair, which they said was otherwise virtually invisible from the street. This story ran in the *Leicester Mercury* on 6 July 1996.

From the country that brought you John Wayne and Humphrey Bogart, a new development: a personal smoke deodoriser. A slew of products aimed at snuffing out smoke odour comes as the backlash against smokers and their fiendish smell reaches new heights. In Los Angeles, a man recently sued his neighbours, complaining that their habit made him ill, and one company in New Hampshire sniff delivery drivers to make sure they haven't smoked on the job. The 'Land of the Free'? Don't make us laugh.

Not that the 'Land of Hope and Glory' has much to shout about. UK sales executive Mark Hodges was sacked on the second day of his job for smoking ... at home. That personal smoke deodoriser might come in handy after all.

Exclusive, smoking saves life

A Spanish doctor once revived a stillborn child by blowing smoke at it. The child began to cough, then to breathe, and was later christened Pablo Picasso.

Shock news, students spend money on booze and fags

A University smoking ban was dropped after students snubbed campus bars, slashing profits by more than £26,000 in thirteen days. Drink takings crashed as students sought alternative venues so they could put away. A check of the books showed one bar lost £15,547, with a 36 per cent fall in sales. Union official Tom Wong said, 'We are one of the biggest tudent unions in the country and we can absorb the cost but we were still shocked to think that students are spending that much money on beer.'

Philip Morris's attempt to curry favour with the smoke police hit trouble when it was argued that millions of anti-smoking book covers sent to teenagers contained 'subliminal' messages telling kids to light up. To the average Joe, the covers showed a teenager flying over a snowy mountain on a snowboard with the hip and trendy message: 'Don't wipe out. Think. Don't smoke.' But it seems that the tobacco companies are even more evil and sinister than everyone thought. 'The snowboard looks like a lit match. The clouds look like smoke. The mountains look like mounds of tobacco at an auction,' raged the director of California's Health Kids Program. Perhaps PM should give up their fruitless toadying to the healthists and stick to what they do best, making cigarettes.

The first woman in England known to smoke cigarettes was Lady Caroline Murdaunt of Walton Hall, Walton-Delvile, Warwickshire in 1858.

In 1998, death-row inmate Larry White was refused his last request, a cigarette, on the grounds that it would have been bad for his health. Now that really *is* disgraceful.

From ABC TV *Eyewitness News*, 12 February 1996: 'In Farmingdale, New York, a man fell into a water tank, breaking just about every bone in his body. In mental as well as physical extremis for half an afternoon as rescuers tried to get to him, he pleaded vainly with a paramedic to give him a cigarette. Afterwards, his "rescuer" boasted to ABC News, "Of course, I didn't do it."' What principles. What a guy.

In 1977 Malcolm Wilding decided to pay his wife back for smoking by wearing a World War Two gas mask at home. The *Sun* newspaper reported that he wore it watching the telly, at the dinner table, and even in bed. He said, 'I've tried everything to make her give up. I'm hoping to embarrass her so much and make her so sick of the sight of the mask she'll chuck the fags.' Wife Liz merely responded by lighting another fag and saying, 'He looks like Darth Vader.'

And here's the same story American-style …

Retired US Army colonel Richard Thomas sued his wife of 43 years for violations under the US Clean Air Act in order to get her to stop smoking. 'Victory is mine,' he crowed, even though he admitted that his wife had given up cigarettes because she was a private person and was upset by the publicity. Now that's what we call a marriage made in heaven.

We hope that when Mrs Thomas makes her will she remembers Robert Brett, who was the first to insert a smoking clause as condition of inheritance. A Californian who wasn't allowed to smoke at home, he left his entire estate to his wife on the condition that she smoked four cigars a day for the rest of her life. He was Havana laugh, wasn't he?

A restaurant is dodging a ban on smoking in all New York eateries by parking a stretch limousine outside its premises for customers to use as a smoking lounge. 'I'm telling you now this is my favourite place,' Victoria Benatar, an architect from Venezuela said. 'There aren't so many smokers left in New York. It is as if you had the plague in Europe in medieval times.' No it's not, Victoria, it's worse.

In 1999 a bill was introduced in the State of Oklahoma banning the sale of pink and blue bubble gum cigars to fathers who wanted to celebrate the birth of their children in a way that didn't involve tobacco. Officious busybody (sorry,

State Representative) Ray Vaughan Redmond proclaimed, 'There should be no non-tobacco item sold in this state designed to resemble tobacco products, including but not limited to big cigars and candy cigarettes.'

Marie Ellis died in December 2004, aged 105, after puffing through 15 cigarettes every day of her adult life. In fact, she was such a prolific smoker that fellow residents at her nursing home sent a wreath to the funeral in the shape of a cigarette. In one newspaper it was reported that Marie was cremated. (We bet she was.)

SOME WIT ABOUT THE WEED ...

I make it a rule never to smoke while I'm sleeping.

Mark Twain

I'm not really a heavy smoker any more. I only get through two lighters a day.

Bill Hicks, American Comedian

If you don't drink, smoke, or drive a car, you are a tax evader.

Thomas S Foley, Politician

I was with some Vietnamese lately, and some of them were smoking two cigarettes at the same time. That's the kind of customers we need!

> **Jesse Helms, Politician**

I've every sympathy with the American who was so horrified by what he had read about the effects of smoking that he gave up reading.

> **Henry G Strauss**

Quitting smoking is easy. I've done it hundreds of times.

> **Mark Twain 1835 - 1910**

New studies show that 100% of all smokers die.

> **Craig Bruce**

Smoking is one of the leading causes of statistics.

> **Fletcher Knebel, 1911- 1993 American historian/novelist**

I phoned my Dad and told him I had stopped smoking. He called me a quitter.

> **Steven Pearl, US Filmmaker**

Is the noble Lord aware that, at my age of 80, there are very few pleasures left to me, but one of them is passive smoking.

> **Baroness Trumpington, former Tory minister and non-smoker in the House of Lords**

I have made it a rule never to smoke more than one cigar at a time.

Mark Twain

It's 106 miles to Chicago, we got a full tank of gas, half a pack of cigarettes, it's dark and we're wearing sunglasses.
Hit it!

Blues Brothers

And a woman is only a woman, but a good cigar is a smoke.

Rudyard Kipling 1865 - 1936

You can't be as old as I am without waking up with a surprised look on your face every morning. 'Holy Christ, whaddya know, I'm still around'! It's absolutely amazing that I survived all the booze, and smoking, and the cars and the career.'

Paul Newman 1925 -

If there are no cigars in heaven I shall not go.

Mark Twain

Pontificating anti-smokers should be reminded that we enjoy relative peace today thanks to servicemen who, in combat and in the trenches, relied for comfort on cigarettes, nearly a billion of which were dispensed in the two world wars.

David Tang - designer

CHAPTER EIGHT

CIG HEIL: THE RISE OF THE SMOKE POLICE

Nobody likes a quitter

'The haunting fear that someone, somewhere, may be happy.'

Definition of Puritanism, H L Mencken

For eleven long years in the 17th century, England was plunged into a culture of organised gloom. From 1649 to 1660 the government, under killjoy Oliver Cromwell, told the famously libertarian English how to conduct their lives, what to eat, what to drink, how to pray and to whom, and how to enjoy themselves (usually by not doing so, as misery was compulsory). Christmas was abolished, theatres were closed and acting became a criminal offence, punishable by whipping. It was a golden age for the sneak and the busybody.

Remind you of anyone?

Welcome to the Brave New World of the 21st-century Puritans. Theatres seem to have survived (for now), but the self-appointed guardians of our moral and physical well-being have turned their obtrusive and unwelcome attention to other areas of private pleasure. It has become increasingly clear that there is no area of our lives that these meddling do-gooders do not aim to control.

Quick! This'll be a no-smoking building when it's finished.

Drinkers, fat people, thin ones too and the pursuers of country sports are frowned upon and tutted at. But nothing rouses their sanctimonious fury more than the smoker. Millions of pounds have been spent on sending squillions of messages to smokers to quit, warning them that smoking is filthy and antisocial, that smokers are endangering themselves and others. Labels on tobacco products thunder out their deadly warnings to the hapless smokers. But still those smokers puff on, to the fury of the health police. Smoking has escalated into a nicotine war, with formidable forces lined up on each side of the battlefield.

So when did the persecution begin? Ominously, for the smoker, almost from the first drag. Rodrigo de Jerez, the first white man to smoke, and the one responsible for bringing tobacco to Europe, also has the unfortunate distinction of being the first devotee of the weed to be banged up for being satanically possessed, by none other than the Spanish Inquisition. History does not reveal whether he chose to resume the habit on his release three years later. Suffice to say that, by that time, tobacco had worked its magic. Smoking had become all the rage in Spain and even the men in red recognised the impracticability of subjecting every last smoker to the bastinado and the rack. What a joy it must have been for them to see their cause taken up with such enthusiasm a century later by the moralising spoilsport and all-round pious little prig James VI of Scotland, newly crowned James I of England.

> **FACT**
> The first tobacco prohibition in history was in Lima in 1588. An ecclesiastical decree ordained: 'It is forbidden under penalty of eternal damnation for a priest to take the smoke tobacco in the mouth, or the powder of tobacco in to the nose, or even under the guise of medicine, before the service of the mass.'

As King of the Scots, James had distinguished himself by ensnaring and torturing those he considered antichrists and Satanists, chalking up a record tally of 400 'witches' burned annually throughout his reign. Fresh from his exertions north of the border, he lost no time in turning his sanctimonious attentions to the evils of tobacco which, in the English, had found the biggest market in Europe.

Haranguing his subjects through a sour little pamphlet entitled 'A Counterblaste to Tobacco', James appealed to the racist in them: 'And now Good Countrymen let us (I pray you) consider, what honour of policy can move us to imitate the barbarous and beastly manners of the wild, God-less and slavish Indians, especially in so vile and stinking a custom? Why do we not as well imitate them in walking naked as they do? In preferring glasses, feathers and such toys to gold and precious stones, as they do? Yea, why do we not deny God and adore the Devil, as they do?'

Just in case they hadn't quite got the picture, he reminded smokers what pathetic losers they really were: 'Have you not reason then to be ashamed, and to forbear this filthy novelty so basely grounded, so foolishly received and so grossly mistaken in the use thereof? A custom loathsome to the eye, hateful to the nose, harmful to the brain, dangerous to the lungs, and in the black stinking fume thereof, nearest resembling the horrible Stygian smoke of the pit that is bottomless.'

An early curtain-raiser to the little darlings at ASH, we're sure you'll agree, but in those dark and unenlightened days people were far more inclined to think for themselves. As much as Elizabeth had been loved and feared, James was disliked and mocked. Apart from the usual court toadies, no one took a blind bit of notice of him and, stamping his little feet in fury, 'the wisest fool in Christendom' raised the duty on tobacco by a spiteful 4,000 per cent. 'That'll show them,' he thought.

But Wee James underestimated his enterprising and free-thinking subjects in a way that his wily predecessor Elizabeth would never have done. Noting that the duty applied only to imports, the English began large-scale domestic cultivation of the weed as vast swathes of Middle England were turned over to tobacco plantations. Combusting with fury, James banned it altogether, issuing anti-baccy proclamations left, right and centre, including one from his death bed in 1624. His achievement was an English coastline swarming with smugglers, a rise in tobacco consumption and a collective V-sign to possibly the most unpopular monarch in British history.

But James's efforts to ban the weed paled into insignificance when compared with the exertions of a couple of his fellow rulers, the first Romanov tsar Michael Feodorovich (1596 – 1645) and Murad IV (1612 – 40), ruler of the Ottoman Empire. These two had no interest whatsoever in discouraging tobacco use by raising taxes. Instead, they favoured what we would know today as direct action.

In Feodorovich's case, his preferred method of deterrence was slitting the lips of smokers, occasionally castrating them into the bargain. The lucky ones were exiled to work in the Siberian salt mines, and provided with the smallest teaspoon he could find to help them with the job. But the Tsar was just playing at it, a tyrannical dilettante when compared with his neighbouring ruler, Murad IV. Known as Murad the Cruel, for reasons we can only guess at, the tobacco-hating sultan wandered the streets of his kingdom in disguise, begging a cigarette from friendly smokers, only to behead them on the spot if they obliged. Judge, jury and executioner rolled into one, he would fetch up on the battlefield, punishing soldiers found enjoying a post–combat fag by hanging, drawing and quartering, or, for added variety, pouring molten lead down their throats. By the time he died at the age of 29 he had murdered 80,000 smoking subjects, a most respectable number when you consider that he was unaided by such useful tools of mass execution as the gas chamber and bomb.

FACT
The 1960s saw the launch of a brand of Turkish cigarettes named (possibly ironically) Murads.

In the light of the above, one has to wonder just what it is about the hapless smoker that inspires such hatred in a certain type of person. Murad the Cruel's justification (not that he needed one) was that a firework display celebrating the birth of his first son had burned down most of his capital, Constantinople. Quite what that had to do with tobacco is anybody's guess, but it didn't stop him, Nero-like, putting out a decree announcing that the fire had been caused by smokers, and ordering the closure of all places where smokers were known to congregate.

In the case of dour, unloved James I, it was rumoured that his insane jealousy of the virile, handsome and celebrated father of smoking, Sir Walter Raleigh, occasioned his detestation of the weed. This and the probability that, in the words of H L Mencken, James had a 'haunting fear that someone, somewhere, may be happy', an uncontrollable fury that so many of his subjects were enjoying something from which he himself derived no pleasure.

But, whatever the tyrants' motives, all their efforts at enforcement proved fruitless. It seemed once the masses had experienced this intoxicating pleasure, neither the threat nor reality of persecution could stop them wanting more. In 1648 Mohammed IV, himself a smoker, repealed Murad's 'laws', while the deservedly named Peter the Great emptied the Siberian mines of smokers and teaspoons in 1700. The English, bored witless by the relentless piety and humbug of the

Puritan years, displayed their usual pragmatism by inviting the exiled son of the beheaded Charles I to deliver them from the bigots and killjoys. Mindful of his father's untimely end, the new monarch King Charles II did not disappoint, bringing with him an open mind, rampant appetite for fun and snuff from France. The Europeans, the Turks and the subject peoples of the Empire smoked on.

FACT
Tobacco was banned five times in Japan between 1609 and 1616 on pain of death, but such was the popularity of the weed that the Shogun's bodyguards risked decapitation to go on puffing. The bans were officially repealed in 1625.

Widespread tolerance of smoking prevailed throughout the 18th century and well into the 19th, due to the following it enjoyed among rich and poor alike (not to mention the immense sums it generated in taxes). 'This vice brings in one hundred million francs a year,' said Louis Napoleon III, when petitioned to ban the habit. 'I will certainly forbid it at once, as soon as you can name a virtue that brings in as much revenue.' In England the murmurings of a few fractious tobacco abstainers resulted in the first segregation of smokers from non-smokers in the House of Commons, but smokers simply used it as an excuse to create a new dandified fashion of smoking jackets and caps, marking them out as purveyors of fun and style.

But, as the century progressed, so the opposition to tobacco grew. Queen Victoria of England loathed the habit, and she forbade even her beloved Albert from smoking in her presence. Although tobacco numbered among its fans such icons of the age as Charles Dickens, Charles Darwin, Benjamin Disraeli and Alfred, Lord Tennyson, the Queen's influence held sway with a rising number of po-faced busybodies. Without warning, the 19th century's very own version of the nanny state reared a very ugly head. All individuals, but especially the duped, defiling and morally defective smoker and drinker, had to be reformed, guided and protected from themselves. The temperance movement was born.

At first it was the evils of alcohol that drove the endeavours of this ghastly gaggle of do-gooders. Drinkers were harangued from pulpits and reminded of their wickedness; worms were immersed in alcohol to show sinners the effect of the demon drink on their bodies; children were frightened into signing pledges of abstinence, witnessed by none other than God Himself, and told that these were binding to the end of their days. But it was only a matter of time before they turned their unwanted attentions to the smoker, and the necessity of showing him the corruption of his ways.

FACT
The Victorians were the first to introduce a minimum age limit for smoking, and introduced chocolate cigars and cigarettes to placate their youngsters until they came of age.

To this end the newly formed British Anti-Tobacco and Anti-Narcotic League published a pamphlet called 'Our Boys and Why They Should Not Smoke'. Smoking, it thundered, not only corrupts morals but leads to heavy drinking and, bizarrely, 'causes fires' (shades of Murad the Cruel here). All the old chestnuts were trotted out by the crusading evangelicals, including the inevitable God-bothering exhortation that wound up the pamphlet: 'May those who read this paper resolve that they will seek to realise the chief end of their being, which is to glorify God, and to love and imitate the Saviour, and that they will have nothing to do with habits so offensive and injurious as the smoking of Tobacco.'

And some fell on stony ground. Perhaps overestimating the strength of God's opposition to booze and fags, the temperance brigade lost its fight to get alcohol and tobacco prohibition on the statute books. Rioting occurred in towns where the hectoring teetotallers had made their presence most felt, and the superb Bishop of Peterborough announced to the Lords: 'I would see England free, better than England sober.' The music halls put it rather differently: 'If you try to tax the poor man's beer, I'll meet you one dark night.' Whatever, Asquith, the prime minister at the time, got the message.

On the other side of the Atlantic the temperance movement had the same take on the wicked influence tobacco exerted on its feeble-minded disciples. It went like this: one puff and you were condemned to live as human flotsam for the rest of your natural. One New York school commissioner wrote: 'The cigarette fiend in time becomes a liar and a thief. He will commit petty thefts to get money to feed his insatiable appetite for nicotine. He lies to his parents, his teachers and his best friends. He neglects his studies and, narcotized by nicotine, sits at his desk half stupefied, his desire for work, his ambition, dulled if not dead.' America's answer to James I finished off: 'Many a bright lad has had his will power weakened, his moral principle sapped, his nervous system wrecked, and his whole life spoiled before he is 17 years old by the detested cigarette.'

The stage was set for the dramatic entrance of the National Anti-Cigarette League of America and its founder, Lucy Page Gaston. Described by one wag as having 'a beardless resemblance to Abraham Lincoln', it is Gaston we have to thank for the term 'coffin nails'. Appalled that cigarette consumption had risen from 20 million a year in 1865 to 4 billion in 1895, LPG sprang into action. She held a series of high-profile anti-cigarette rallies across the land, promoting 'clean living' and railing at smokers to give up their dependence on 'The Little White Slavers', and reform forthwith.

She was joined in her moral crusade by a friend and co-zealot, who gloried in the name of Carry A Nation. Nation was a notorious anti-alcohol giantess whose speciality was smashing up gin joints in Kansas with her trademark hatchet. But she also really hated smoking. In her autobiography, hilariously titled *The Use and Need of the Life of Carry A Nation*, she made her views abundantly clear: 'Oh, the vile cigarette. What smell can be worse and more poisonous? I feel outraged at being compelled to smell this poison in the street. I have the right to take cigars and cigarettes from men's mouths in self defense.'

At first these two charmers seemed to be making progress. Cigarette production dropped from 4.9 billion in 1897 to 2.5 billion in 1901 and they went on to achieve a myriad of laws against smoking including one in New York, passed in 1908, prohibiting women from smoking in public. But, evidently unaware of the truism that the more you try to stamp out a vice, the more attractive it becomes, their fanatical condemnation of tobacco eventually contributed to more smoking, not less. In 1910 cigarette sales reached 8 billion and,

Carry A Nation: 'Oh the vile cigarette. What smell can be worse and more poisonous?'

one by one, the laws Gaston and Nation had lobbied to achieve were repealed. The same year Carry A Nation's career as an anti-vice crusader ended while rolling down stairs, courtesy of a punch thrown by a whorehouse madam, and she died of unrelated injuries shortly after in a Kansas mental institution.

Gaston carried on her crusade alone, standing for president in 1921 on a clean morals ticket, and was aghast when Warren Harding, a cigarette smoker, beat her to the White House. Expressing the highly Christian view that he would die in office, she was delighted to see her prediction fulfilled in 1923, only to have her glee cut short when she was struck by a trolley bus (we can only hope this was not deliberate). She died soon after, not from her injuries but from throat cancer, having never smoked nor tolerated smoking in her presence. When she founded the National Anti-Smoking League, 4 billion cigarettes

> *'O ye wha are sae guid yourself*
> *Sae pious and sae holy*
> *Ye've noght to do but mark and tell*
> *Your neibours' fauts and folly.'*
>
> *'Address to the Rigidly Righteous' by Robbie Burns,*
> *poet, smoker, all-round bad boy, and author of*
> *'Nine Inch Will Please a Lady'*

were sold annually. In the year she died, a Gaston-busting 73 billion cigarettes were consumed by the great American public.

At this juncture it is worth noting the disastrous consequences of the prohibition of tobacco's comrade-in-arms and fellow-vice, alcohol. In 1919 the US temperance movement achieved its most longed-for aim: the Eighteenth Amendment to the Constitution was ratified, allowing a Federal prohibition of booze. 'The reign of tears is over,' said the evangelist Billy Sunday. 'The slums will soon only be a memory. Men will walk upright now, women will smile and the children will laugh. Hell will be forever for rent.' Delirious with triumph, the canting bigot added: 'Prohibition is won, now for tobacco.' The American public replied by consuming over 100 billion cigarettes for the first time in tobacco's history. Hallelujah.

Tobacco had given *its* answer. But Sunday's verdict on the demise of the demon drink also proved premature. Within ten years, more than half a million Americans had been arrested for violation of the anti-alcohol laws and 35,000 had died from alcohol poisoning. Moreover, the beverage industry had fallen into the hands of organised crime and found a natural home alongside gambling and

prostitution. After the most disastrous attempt a
social engineering in America's history, the
Prohibition laws were repealed in 1933.

Having seen off the temperance movement
tobacco started the 1930s in pretty good shape
throughout the world. True, a few peevish busybodie
had made themselves disagreeable now and again
but, on the whole, any organised hostility to the
weed had been seen off in style. But, until now, the
opposition had stood largely on a religious platform
emphasising the moral delinquency and feeble-
mindedness of smokers and drinkers. Now the anti
added health to the agenda.

As early as 1907, the British Medical Association
highlighted the risk of cancer of the lip (althougl
this was hotly contested by Parisian scientists in 192.
who claimed that smoking was beneficial). Ir
Germany, from the late 1920s onwards, Dr Frit:
Lickint (who was first to coin the term 'passive
smoking') published a series of reviews of smoking
which left no doubt that tobacco smoke was a majo.
cause of lung cancer. It was at this point that the
Nazis entered the smoking arena.

Until the health police gained ascendancy ir
Western democracies in the late 20th century, the
Nazi government had held sway as implementing the

most invasive public health policies ever seen. Cancer was declared 'the number-one enemy of the State', and people were exhorted to rid their diets of fat, sugar and alcohol in favour of natural foods such as whole-grain bread coupled with communal compulsory physical exercise. (Sounds familiar, doesn't it.) Nazi Germany became a transparent society, not in a democratic sense, but one in which the lives of its citizens were on show at all times, illustrated in a 1938 law forbidding attic storage. Thousands of 'registered' alcoholics were arrested and sterilised under the Law for the Prevention of Genetically Diseased Offspring. The aim was to create an Aryan master race, living to healthy immortality in an orderly and sterile Utopia.

It is well known that the shrieking little man with the Charlie Chaplin moustache was rabidly anti-smoking, his proud boast being that he had 'tossed his cigarettes into the Danube and never reached for them again'. The person who brought more misery to the world than any other joined the distinguished ranks of James I, Murad the Cruel and Lucy PG, throwing his weight enthusiastically behind the campaign against cigarette smoking. One magazine slathered sycophantically: 'Brother socialist, do you know that our Führer is against smoking and thinks that every German is responsible to the whole people for all his deeds and emissions, and does not have the right to damage his body with drugs.' It is less well known that, while Hitler was advocating body cleansing and detox, he was popping pills of every size and colour, a fact kept very much under wraps in his 'transparent society'.

Adolf's main cheerleader in the crusade to ban smoking was Leonardo Conti, a strong anti-tobacco activist who was rewarded for his toadying with the plum job of Reich Health Führer. A dedicated Nazi, who cheated justice by hanging himself in his cell at Nuremberg, Conti created the Bureau against the Dangers of Alcohol and Tobacco, which enforced strict anti-smoking controls. Tobacco was attacked as a 'relic of a liberal lifestyle' and as a 'masturbation of the lungs'. Draconian restrictions were placed on advertising and a typically restrained National Socialist poster campaign was launched showing a Nazi jackboot stamping on a smoker's head. Women were banned from buying cigarettes. 'The German woman does not smoke,' proclaimed a Nazi slogan. But, despite the widespread propaganda against the drug dubbed 'genetic poison' by the Racial Hygiene movement, all did not go according to plan.

Although the tragically obedient Germans

appeared happy to be force-fed a diet of swastikas and moral squalor, when it came to tobacco, the threats, propaganda and intense health promotion activity resulted in dismal failure. In 1939 the Berlin correspondent of the American Medical Association gleefully reported that cigarette consumption had increased from 609 to 676 per capita in just one year. Adolf hit back. In 1942, he formed the Institute for the Struggle against the Dangers of Tobacco, and dictated that cigarettes be distributed to soldiers 'in a manner that would dissuade them from excessive smoking'. Consequently, a solider risking his life for the Vater Land in sub-zero temperatures thousands of miles away from his loved ones had the nicotinal consolation of just six cigarettes a day.

One of Hitler's priceless swanks was that 'Germany might never have achieved its present glory' if he had continued to smoke. In 1945, along with other boastful claims, this assertion lay in ruins, like his country. As the corpse of the Supreme Warlord lay sizzling on a rubbish tip outside his Berlin bunker, all his remaining staff inside lit up, something that in his lifetime had been expressly forbidden. Faced with all the problems left to them by their Führer and with the Russian Army raping and pillaging two streets away, they reached for the comfort of a fag.

But, somewhere in hell, the little corporal was to have the last laugh. In death Hitler achieved his heart's desire of all but expunging the weed from German life, but not in the glorious way he'd intended. With their cigarette industry operating at only 10 per cent of its pre-war levels, the tobacco-starved Germans were forced to grow the stuff in their window boxes. The government allowed some tobacco cultivation but, hey, this was Germany, and only 25 plants were permitted tax free and only 200 per individual. Old Nazi habits died hard and the smoke police enforced these restrictions with all the time-honoured rigour and enthusiasm of the officially redundant Third Reich.

Elsewhere, tobacco's fortunes had fared rather better. While Hitler was praying to the health god, Winston Churchill, Roosevelt and Stalin all smoked, not only permitting the weed to their troops but giving it the same importance as medical supplies. In Churchill's case, its importance symbolised far more than one man's pleasure. Understanding every bit as well as Hitler the power of propaganda, Churchill exploited to the full his famous 'V for victory' sign with a cigar of gigantic proportions tucked between his fingers, as inseparable from a symbol of freedom as his vegetarian, teetotalling anti-smoking opponent was from the jackboot.

With or without Churchill, the post-war cigarette industry went from strength to strength, about 80 per cent of all men in Britain smoked, along with 40 per cent of women, and the biggest market research project ever undertaken was set up to document such habits in the lives of the working man and woman. Creepily named the 'Mass Observation' programme, this was a curious little exercise in which 'observers' went undercover to spy on the working class at play in the town of Bolton, thinly disguised as 'Worktown'. Unsurprisingly, the survey confirmed anthropologists' fears that vast quantities of tobacco and alcohol featured in their lives and, not for the first time, there were ominous rumblings from on high that these unhealthy proles must be straightened up and made to behave.

But, although medical research increasingly linked smoking to lung cancer, it was not yet considered the role of government to limit tobacco by legislation. In 1954, Health Minister Iain Macleod walked into a press conference, lit up a cigarette and announced that a government scientific committee had concluded that smoking causes lung cancer. He thanked Richard Doll at the Medical Research Council for 'what little information we have' and continued to chain-smoke throughout the conference. It was not until 1962 that the British government (or any government, come to that) took it upon itself to advise its citizens to desist from smoking on health grounds. This signalled the real start of the tobacco wars, lighting up was never to be the same again.

Since then there have been an estimated 60,000 studies saying that smoking is bad for you, and this is quite possibly a conservative estimate. Current anti-smoking research states that 5 million people a year die from smoking, a figure disputed by pro-smokers who say that smoking is being made the scapegoat for conditions such as poor diet, obesity, stress and diabetes. An article in 1988 called 'Lies, Damned Lies and 400,000 Smoking Related Deaths' claimed that 'The war on smoking has grown into a monster of deceit and greed, eroding the credibility of government and subverting the rule of law.'

This would seem to be borne out when, in 1990, Stanton Glantz, Professor of Cardiology at California University, made a revealing little speech at an anti-smoking conference in Australia: 'The main thing that science has done on the issue of ETS in addition to help people like me to pay mortgages, is it has legitimised the concerns that people have that they don't like cigarette smoke. And that is a strong emotional force that needs to be harnessed and used.

There we have it, straight from the horse's mouth, well, that of a prominent anti-smoker anyway. The 'science' of passive smoking keeps him in his chosen style of living, and can be used as an 'emotional' tool to stir up intolerance in people who simply dislike the smell of smoke. Glantz finished his speech with an unscientific cry of triumph: 'We're on a roll and the bastards are on the run.' It would appear, then, that the issue of passive smoking is a fantastic way of turning smokers into social outcasts and objects of hate, too.

Whatever the accuracy or otherwise of the research on offer, there is no doubt that today's debates about health are often thinly disguised moral judgements on people's lifestyle and behaviour, a continual interference in private matters that are no concern of the State. In, New York, famously named 'The City That Never Sleeps', Mayor Michael Bloomberg has imposed his edict on every bar, hotel, restaurant and club. Where once its inhabitants revelled in its 24-hour-a-day pleasures, smokers have become lepers with nowhere to go but the streets. Defending his draconian legislation, Bloomberg compared the actions of smokers to those of the terrorists who murdered thousands of innocent people by ramming their planes into the World Trade Center. 'Think about all the press attention to 9/11,' he said. 'That number of people die every year in the city from second-hand smoke … it's *literally* [our italics] true that something like a thousand people will not die each year that would have otherwise died.'

It is to her credit that the rabidly anti-smoking Dr Elizabeth Whelan, President of the American Council on Science and Health, spoke out in protest against this vile statement: 'The estimate of the number of deaths prevented is patently absurd. Our best estimate is between zero and a hypothetical ten to fifteen. There is no evidence that any New Yorker, patron or employee, has ever died as a result of exposure to smoke in a bar or restaurant. The majority of New Yorkers will welcome a smoking ban primarily for aesthetic reasons, not for health reasons.'

Yet, on the basis of these lies, this mediocre little bureaucrat has turned the Big Apple, that hitherto beloved bastion of free-thinking optimism, into a city that would close its doors to Churchill and open them to Hitler, and where possession of an unused ashtray stored in a closet at a place of business is a crime.

Aha. Those names again: one that conjures up the idea of good times spent with a drinking, smoking *bon viveur* who valued freedom above all things; the other the vision of a future that Orwell described in

1984 as 'a boot stamping on a human face, forever'. There are those who throw up their hands every time the aims and methods of today's anti-smoking movement are compared with those of German National Socialists. But why? Try and have a debate about passive smoking these days and, unless you agree with the 'research' that it kills anything from x thousand to x million a year, people look at you as if you are denying the Holocaust. Yet in 1998, after spending years and millions on anti-tobacco campaigns and research, the World Health Organisation was forced to admit it had withheld a report showing there was absolutely no link between passive smoking and lung cancer. The tobacco giants have been rightly vilified in the past for such practice.

Suppression of free debate and tobacco advertising bans are not the only parallel with the Nazis' attitude to health. The new health fascists have adopted many, if not all, of the Third Reich pronouncements on public health and lifestyle, namely 'to eat whole-grain bread, fruit and vegetables, to drink mineral water and not beer, and to exercise'. Throw in vegetarianism, animal rights and the imminent appearance of the anti-smoking patrols in our pubs and restaurants and the comparison is complete.

Once, public health was characterised by laudable

> *'The most pernicious thing about smokism is that it is not really about smoking at all. Cigarettes happen to be the product the smokists currently want stamped out. Tomorrow it could be, and will be, white bread, or beer, or junk food, or mashed potatoes. The object of the exercise is to impose the will of those who believe they know best on a supine population which is supposed not to know enough to come in out of the rain.'*
>
> *Keith Waterhouse, 'Filter Tip of the Iceberg', the Mirror, 24 April 1986*

concern about sanitation and contagious disease. The 21st century has seen its role reduced to self-righteous attacks on politically incorrect lifestyles of which those in power do not approve. Truly the Nazi slogan 'Health is not a private matter' has found its natural home in New Labour's Britain.

So what does the future hold? A Western society cleansed of tobacco, alcohol and saturated fats, where children grow up in a spotless environment free from any hazard, where all health choices have been made for you so that you don't have to do it yourself, and where lawyers queue up to sue anything containing calories. A society where you can be jailed for smoking in front of your children, in which you can be sacked from your job for smoking at home, and where a smoker is deemed unworthy to be a public servant. No, wait, sorry, that's not the future, that's the present.

The great historian A J P Taylor wrote in 1965 that: 'The British people had set out to destroy Hitler and National Socialism, "Victory at all costs". Yet they remained a peaceful and civilised people, tolerant, patient and generous' (*English History, 1914–1945*). One of the many depressing aspects of the current appetite for banning things is that so many of our countrymen approve of the impositions by the few on millions of their fellow citizens. Even worse, some are indifferent. 'Civilised'? 'Tolerant'? 'Generous'? Wherever did it all go wrong?

Individual choice is a fundamental right. There is no doubt that those who cleave to that point of view will be drawn to others that do so, and will buck the system that lectures and hectors. Let's hope there are enough people left to reach for the fags and blow smoke in the eyes of the self-appointed moralists with their arrogant disregard for civil liberties. Smokers and their evil counterparts, drinkers, are sociable coves and unofficial members of the Naughty Club, comrades in arms. Long may they flourish.

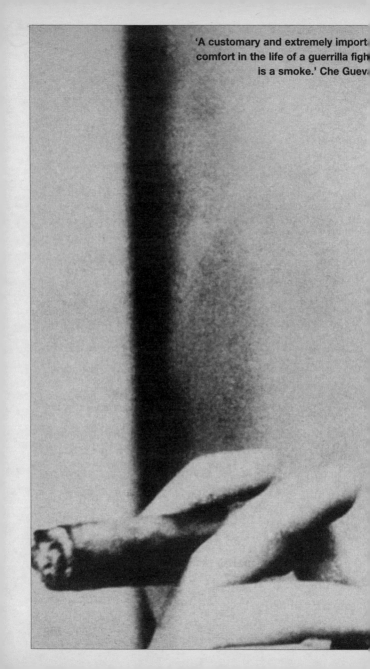

'A customary and extremely important comfort in the life of a guerrilla fighter is a smoke.' Che Guevara

THE MOST IRRITATING THINGS YOU CAN SAY TO A SMOKER

1. Just think of all the money you could be saving
2. It's very ageing you know
3. You want to give that up, love
4. Didn't I say, this is a no-smoking house
5. I wouldn't have put you down as a smoker
6. You smoke HOW MANY?
7. I gave up six hundred days, eight hours and four seconds ago – still miss 'em
8. I hate to imagine the state of your lungs ...
9. Do you know, you smell like an ashtray
10. You must have money to burn
11. Did you smoke all of those? (pointing to ashtray)
12. Not another bloody smoker. I'm going to end up with lung cancer

CHAPTER NINE

CIGGIE STARDUSTS: FAME AND CIGARETTES

Smoking skills

'I used to smoke two packs a day and I just hate being a non-smoker, because I always find smokers the most interesting people on the table.'
Michelle Pfeiffer

'If I have to go before my time, this is how I'll go, a cigarette in one hand, glass of scotch in the other.'

Ava Gardner

Musician Joe Jackson quit New York after two decades because he couldn't cope in a city that no longer smokes. The ab fab Joanna Lumley says she smokes from 'none to twenty' a day and Anna Friel walked out of the Canadian Embassy when she discovered a smoking ban was imposed on a launch party for a movie premiere. (She was snapped having a ciggie in the doorway.) Princess Margaret couldn't stop, but Camilla Parker-Bowles has resisted her favourite brand since moving into Clarence House with Prince Charles. Or has she? The Prince of Wales can't stop his son Harry from indulging. But then he's not the only royal rebel. Princess Stephanie of Monaco was expelled from school after being caught with a fag. Let's not forget Sarah Ferguson and her covert ciggies either. Comedian Johnny Vegas can't go on stage without one and Dale Winton would only undergo cosmetic surgery when he found a surgeon who would allow him to have a pre-op cigarette. In 2004, five out of the ten *I'm A Celebrity Get Me Out Of Here* contestants smoked while in the jungle. Geri Halliwell has been pictured smoking and Tara Palmer-Tomkinson, although she's quit drugs and alcohol, says she feels insecure without a pack in her designer handbag. Designer Donatella Versace is such a nicotine fiend that she employs a personal assistant to carry an ashtray for her. Supermodel Naomi Campbell smokes and so does Eva Herzigova, who wears a pair of fine leather gloves when smoking to keep her hands clean and fragrant (natch). When Simon Le Bon met model Yasmin she told him she smoked Marlboro Reds and drank Glenfiddich, so he turned up at her place the next day with a carton of fags and a bottle of Scotch; they wed not long after. Celebrity Chef Marco Pierre White can't resist a cigar, and fellow cook Anthony Worrall Thomson is a patron of pro-smoking group Forest. Actress Julie Goodyear (*Coronation Street*'s Bet Lynch) is a veteran smoker who uses a holder, and in rival show *EastEnders* June Brown (aka Dot Branning) boasts that at 68 she's a forty-a-day woman and proud of it. Asked what she would do if a comet crashed to earth, Tea Leoni said she would smoke as many cigarettes as possible.

And they're far from being the only high-profile celebs whose love affair with tobacco indicates they won't be browbeaten by the anti-smoking lobby:

Jeremy Irons: Actor
'I might smoke more.'

Julian Clary: Comedian
'Sometimes I run around Regent's Park and go to the gym. I can manage about half an hour, but must stop for a cigarette every so often.'

Nicki Haslam: Designer
'My doctor phoned and said, "You don't deserve this news but your lungs are crystal clear."'

Freddie Starr: Comedian
'I've been smoking thirty years now. And there's nothing wrong with my lung.'

David Hockney: Artist
'Frankly I think that New Labour is inherently bossy. Smoking is my affair, not the Blairs'. It has nothing to do with them. I read that the Queen allows smoking

at lunch and I thought, well, of course the Queen wouldn't be telling people not to smoke. She's far too polite. I don't believe the stuff about second-hand smoke; I don't believe a lot of the stuff from medical people. When the health people say you would be healthier if you don't smoke, they don't know that because they don't know what would replace it. What the health people ignore is the fickle finger of fate. Something is going to kill me. Actually, I think smoking is rather good for me. And it's enjoyable. A little bit of what you fancy does you good.'

Anthony Worrall Thompson: TV chef and restaurateur

'One has to stand up to the more extreme anti-smokers because they aren't representative of the public as a whole. If I wanted to live in an intolerant, smoke-free universe I'd move to California, but I don't and nor do millions of other people.'

Jeremy Clarkson: Writer/TV presenter

'Smokers pay £19,000 a minute to the Exchequer, and that's enough to pay for the whole police force. Or to put it another way, for every £1 we cost the NHS we give it £3.60. Please don't encourage the state to dictate how I live my life.'

177

Johnny Depp: Film star

(To an American lady who complained about his smoking in London restaurant Scalinis):

'I'm sorry, but we're not in LA now.'

Dale Winton: TV presenter

'On the eve of my cosmetic surgery operation my doctor said to me, "No food, cigarettes or alcohol after eight o'clock tonight." The no-alcohol rule wasn't a problem for me but the ban on cigarettes certainly was. That night I walked through the Swiss town of Fribourg and was having second thoughts. I sat down had a coffee and automatically lit a cigarette. At that very moment my doctor walked by, catching me red-handed. So I smoked another one.'

Brian Conley: Actor/comedian

'If I haven't got a cigarette I smell my fingers, just to get a whiff of lingering nicotine.'

Groucho Marx: A woman is an occasional
pleasure but a cigar is always a smoke.

178

SNUFFED IT: GREAT SMOKERS GONE BUT NOT FORGOTTEN

Chairman Mao
Marlene Dietrich
Albert Einstein
Johnny Cash
Winston Churchill
Josef Stalin
Jimmy Durante
George Orwell
Lucille Ball
Sammy Davis Jr
Al Capone
Che Guevara
John Lennon
Lord Alfred Tennyson
Compton Mackenzie
James Dean
Al Jonson
Tallulah Bankhead
Carole Lombard
John Wayne
Walt Disney
Orson Welles
Robert Mitchum
Lana Turner
Joan Crawford
George Sanders
Franklin D Roosevelt
Fats Waller
David Niven

Dennis Potter
Yul Brynner
Mark Twain
Josef Stalin
Betty Grable
Bette Davis
Humphrey Bogart
Nat 'King' Cole
Noel Coward
Sir John Gielgud
Sigmund Freud
Steve McQueen
Spencer Tracy
Alfred Hitchcock
Oscar Wilde
Princess Margaret
Lord Byron
Karl Marx
Groucho Marx
Frank Sinatra
George Burns
James Cagney
PG Wodehouse
Sir Laurence Olivier
Betty Grable
Dorothy Lamour
Bing Crosby
Jackie Kennedy
Susan Hayward
Audrey Hepburn
Simone Signoret
Ava Gardner

Joe Jackson: Musician

'I'm a moderate smoker myself; I enjoy a couple o
cigarettes or a cigar with a drink. But I'm also
health-conscious person and, over the past few years
I've done extensive research into all sides of th
smoking issue. I've concluded that smoking is risk
but not as dangerous as zealous officials and anti
smoking activists would have us believe. More t
the point, I'm convinced (as are many reputabl
scientists) that the danger of "passive smoking"
is pretty much a hoax, with dodgy statistic
manipulated and exaggerated with the expres
intention of stigmatising smokers and scaring the hel
out of everyone.'

Tommy Walsh: *Ground Force* gardener

'I used to smoke all the time but four years ago
changed my smoking habit to smoke only when I'n
drinking. However, this policy has had an advers
effect on my drinking habits.'

Robert Elms: Style guru

'I'm sorry, but our bodies are not temples, they'r
pleasure palaces to be enjoyed. I know smokin
is bad for your health; I'm very glad I don't do i
but I'm gladder still that we live in a place wher

people can make adult, informed choices about their own lifestyles.'

Bill Wyman

'I smoke, I eat a lot of red meat, have loads of sugar and loads of salt.'

And there are plenty of female pro-smoker celebs too:

Amanda Donahoe: Actress

'Smoking and red wine go hand in hand and are among life's little pleasures. I mean, nowadays there are a lot of things you're not supposed to eat and even sex is dangerous. I just think, Blow it. I'll probably get knocked down by a bus anyway.'

Kate Winslet: Actress

'I'm a hardened Brit. I cannot do without my nicotine habit and caffeine.'

Emmylou Harris: Singer

'I didn't start smoking till I was in my early forties. So I think I can smoke moderately now for twenty years and deal with it later.'

THEY'RE ANTI SMOKING: IS THIS A CLUB YOU'D WANT TO JOIN?

Ken Livingstone
Cherie Blair
Edwina Currie
Adolf Hitler
Mayor Bloomberg
The Spanish Inquisition
Carole Caplin
Anne Diamond
Lucy Page Gaston
James I
Murad the Cruel
Janet Street-Porter

Joanna Lumley: Actress/writer

'I like smoking, anything between none and twenty a day.'

Anna Friel: Actress

'I don't expect special treatment, but to be thrown out into the cold every time I want a sneaky cigarette is a bit much.'

Kate Moss: Model

'Because I'm pictured smoking I'm blamed not only for anorexia but lung cancer. This lady from the American Cancer Association told the *New York*

Daily News that I was a bad role model for teenage girls, and then I see it on TV, they're doing a big show on it: "Are these girls bad role models?" People like Sylvester Stallone or Arnold Schwarzenegger go through films killing hundreds of people and then they turn round and call me a bad role model because I smoke.'

Sharon Stone: Film star

'You shouldn't do bad things to excess, but it's good to have a drink now and then. Good to have a steak and smoke a cigarette.'

Diana Rigg: Actress

'I smoke and I drink and I don't do gyms. I do adore all the good things in life.'

Joan Collins: Actress/author

'I drink wine, I stay up late, eat chocolate and smoke cigarettes. A doctor told me once that smoking less than seven cigarettes was the same as breathing in the exhaust fumes of all the lorries on the streets. So stay indoors and carry on tabbing.

Goldie Hawn: Film star

'I have all the vices: I smoke and I eat.'

Anna Kournikova: Tennis player

'I live for the moment. If I want to eat this kind of thing I do. If I want a cigarette I have one. Life is for living, you only get it once.'

Joni Mitchell: Singer/songwriter

'I started smoking at the age of nine. I had polio and when I got out of hospital I kind of made a pact with my Christmas tree, or maybe it was God, that if I could get my legs back … But I had this debt to pay back because I did stand up, unfurl and walk. So I joined the church choir and one night after choir practice in the middle of winter a girl had snitched a pack of Black Cats from her mother and we all sat in the wintry fish pond in the snow and we passed them around. And you know, some girls choked and some threw up, and I took one puff and I felt really smart. I just thought, Woah. My head cleared up. I seemed to see better and think better. So I was a smoker from that day on, secretly, covertly. And I'm still smoking.'

Marianne Faithfull: Singer

'One of the reasons I have to sleep a lot is that when I'm asleep I'm not smoking.'

ab C Nesbitt: There are many reasons why cigs are a good
ing. This is not one of them…

while this is. Joan Alone – Ms Collins turns to a fag
comfort.

What a drag it is getting old ... Mick Jagger with Keith
Richards and his little helper (*top*).

A hard day's light ... John Lennon wants something stronger
(*bottom*)

iggy Stardust (*top*) ... David Bowie, the man who smoked
e world.

oel and Liam Gallagher (*bottom left*) enjoy their Cigarettes
d Alcohol

s a long ash is gonna fall – Bob Dylan (*bottom right*)

Sing when you're smoking ... Robbie Williams has a puff.

mme a match ... Blue Liam quits the game for a smoke.

Frock Horror! Enter Dot.

die quits smoking? All Betts are off for Goodyear.

Model behaviour? Kate Moss enjoys a smoke … but not always, and Jodie's not kidding us (*opposite, top*).

b Fab? 'ave tab, darling. Joanna Lumley goes for the Femme
tale look (*bottom left*)

sh show you who I am.' Princess Margaret lights up (in) a
om … (*bottom right*).

Diana Dors: 'Size matters, huh?'

ter O'Toole's philosophy: The glass is half full, the cig is
lf smoked.

Oliver Reed didn't smoke, but his hair soon would … (*top*)
The King-size and I ... Yul Brynner baldly puffs (*bottom left*)
while 50s heartthrob Louis Jordan always had two on the go
once (*right*).

ranco Zeffirelli. The Director's Silk Cut?

Michael Caine. Not many people know this ...

ndy Capp. Tabs, fags, baccy, double yankees, bar-room biffs ...
o smokin' pet, no jokin'.

'More of your finest toxin, please, waiter!' Jeremy Clarkson leaves the car at home.

Drew Barrymore: Actress

'If there could be an alcoholic word for smoking then that would be me. I'm a smokaholic. I love everything about smoking. I love that it cures my oral fixations. I love that it's something to do. It's something in my hand. I like the smell of it, the taste of it. I love the first cigarette in the morning. I love the last one before I go to bed and every one in between. If I could, I would smoke and eat at the same time. If it's a fault, it's definitely one I take pride in.'

Geri Halliwell: Singer

'It's my New Year's resolution, I started smoking again.'

Jeanne Moreau: Actress

'I resist giving up cigarettes because it's forbidden. Do you know what I mean? I don't like the idea of me giving up just because other people decide for me.'

Melanie Griffith: Actress

'Yes, I do smoke. And I like it. Hell, yes. And I go into the bathrooms on airplanes and I smoke there.'

Lisa Stansfield: Singer

'I've tried giving up twice but then I became the bitch from hell. Unconsciously, I think I do it on purpose. You want someone to turn round and say, "For God's sake, have a cigarette."'

Julia Sawalha: Actress

'Smoking's the last thing I'm going to give up. I've already given up my favourite foods and cut down on alcohol. I really enjoy smoking. I've tried giving up but none of it has worked. I used to rip off the patch at the end of the day so I could have a fag.'

Liz Hurley: Model/actress

'I like my wine and I smoke and my idea of exercise is walking the dog.'

Kate Beckinsale: Actress

'I try and take a lot of vitamins. I don't drink. I do smoke though. I'd be insufferable if I didn't smoke. You'd have to push me off a balcony I'd be so boring.'

Liv Tyler: Actress

'I know I shouldn't smoke but they're so yummy.'

Grace Slick: Singer

'I can imagine myself without everything except cigarettes and a car. I smoke every minute that I'm awake and I have since I was fifteen.'

Kathy Burke: Actress/director

'Yeah babe, you just watch. When I die they'll all blame the fried egg sandwiches and the fags and it'll have been all the fucking wholemeal toast and fresh vegetables.'

Sophie Dahl: Model

'This no smoking in New York. It's like being back at school; one is constantly looking for a suitable bike shed.'

Ellen Barkin: Film star

'I like to see a man smoke one [cigar]. They're so sexy on a man. That's all there is to it.'

Cybill Shepherd: Comedian/actress

'I can smoke with the boys. I've paid my dues and I think women should be able to do anything they can do and do it better.'

TOP 10 SMOKING TOWNS IN BRITAIN

1. Gamesley, Glossop
2. Anundel, Liverpool
3. Nechells, Birmingham
4. Castle, Northampton
5. West City, Newcastle
6. Sparbrook, Birmingham
7. Spinney Hills, Leicester
8. Arboretum, Derby
9. Byker, Newcastle
10. City and Holbeck, Leeds

BOTTOM 10 SMOKING TOWNS IN BRITAIN

1. Great Hollands North, Bracknell
2. Westbrook, Warrington
3. Molesey South, West Molesey
4. The Astons and Heyford, Bicester
5. Great Notley & Braintree West, Braintree
6. South Woodham – Chetwood, Chelmsford
7. Georgeham & Mortehoe, Woodacombe
8. Haydon Wick, Swindon
9. Hawks Green, Cannock
10. Cheam, Sutton

Lisa Marie Presley: Daughter of Elvis

'I smoke. I don't do yoga. I don't meditate or do macrobiotics. I bite the hell out of my nails.'

Victoria Coren: Journalist

'My inspiration has always been Jeanne Calment, a Frenchwoman who smoked and drank every day and died a few years ago at the age of 122. When asked the secret of her longevity, she replied: "I laugh a lot." Well, you would, wouldn't you?'

Chloe Sevigny: Model/actress

'The new smoking ban is discouraging. I think people should have more cocktail parties now they can't smoke in bars.'

CHAPTER TEN

MY MOST MEMORABLE SMOKE

They're
g-g-great

For some smokers it's the first, desperate drag after a long-haul flight. It's no coincidence that for many people a cigarette is the celebration of a job well done, we've lost count of the number of women we've come across who gleefully admitted the most joyous ciggie came immediately after giving birth. 'All I could think of after having my daughter,' said journalist Lynn Barber, 'was a cigarette.' Here celebrities tell us about the best, or worst, smoke of their lives.

Paul O'Grady: Actor/Comedian

'Without a doubt my best ciggie is the Lambert & Butler that gets me out of bed every day. I take that first drag, my eyes cross, the blood pressure rises to 2,000 and it's lovely. Some people reach for a bottle; with me, it's cigarettes, I use them like a dummy. All this nonsense about smoke bans make me sick; it's like rearranging deckchairs on the *Titanic*. And the way people stare when you light up, talk about dirty looks, anyone would think it was crack cocaine you were taking. The truth is that smokers are always courteous. I wouldn't dream of smoking in anyone's car or home. And I always ask politely in public places. The most miserable I've ever been in my life is when I packed in smoking. I've tried every aversion therapy, hypnosis, sniffing pots of old ciggies, nicotine patches. At one point I was patched up like a busted lilo. If it was a choice between a cuppa or a cigarette of a morning the tobacco would win hands down.'

Amanda Barrie: Actress

'I was waiting for my friend, the artist Maggie Hamilton, in my favourite London restaurant, Joe Allen. She likes to eat early, but, for once, I'd arrived before her. I was told that my usual table was occupied, so I sat at the bar. I was enjoying a cigarette when I looked over and saw the person sitting at my table was the American comedian Bea Arthur. A heroine of mine. I don't usually gush, but decided when she got up to leave I just had to tell her I thought she was wonderful, and how, over the years, she's brought so much joy to me and countless others with her brilliantly funny and inspired performances. I reasoned that, after all, I'd always been delighted when people complimented me. I'm not twelve, but as the moment approached I got quite nervous, in fact I think I smoked more than usual. As she got up from her table, dressed in a smart tweed suit, she approached me. "Do I know you?" she bellowed. I went across to greet her, blissfully unaware that I'd not extinguished my cigarette, the end of which was blazing with a red hot cinder waiting to drop. Planning to explain that we did indeed have a mutual friend I went to embrace her and the next thing I know is that I'm furiously trying to stop the legendary Bea Arthur going up in flames. I'd managed to put my cigarette out … on her. I think she thought I was some pyromaniac, loony fan. Needless to say we didn't become best mates. I will never forget that cigarette.

Do I still smoke? You bet.'

Dale Winton: TV Presenter

'The cigarette after sex takes some beating. On one occasion, though, I remember what should have been the best cig turned out to be the worst. It was in 1994, January, freezing cold and when I went to light up, after marvellous sex, the man I was with demanded I smoke outside. So there I was, having put my heart and soul into making this person as happy as I could, chucked out of bed and relegated to puffing away at 1am on the patio. I could not believe it. I'm a natural rebel and there's nothing worse than telling me I can't do something. Needless to say that was the end of that relationship. The next best smoke to the one after sex is the cigarette after a long-haul flight. I long for the moment the "fasten your seatbelt" sign comes on just knowing that beneath us is the joy of 10,000 ashtrays.'

Brian Conley: Actor/Comedian

'I'm a forty-a-day man. In fact, I'll say to people, "Get that food out of my face, I'm trying to have a fag." Of course, over the years we've all become sensitive to the needs of non-smokers, especially at big venues like the Albert Hall. It was here, where I was touring with Bob Hope, that I had what had to be my most memorable cigarette. I'd gone outside the building for a quick puff and stood under a window. Unknown to me it was Bob Hope's dressing room and he called me over. He, it turned out, was enjoying a cigar and was appalled to see me having to lurk outside. I was summoned in and found myself chatting to the man himself, a living legend. Apparently he'd seen me in the West End production of *Me and My Girl*. "How old are you?" he asked. "Thirty-four," I replied. "My boy," he said, drawing on a huge Havana, "you've got it all."

'Much later, I was asked to do a tribute for him at a showbiz "roasting" in celebration of his career and, when a *This Is Your Life* was done on Bob, I was invited along. All because I had that cigarette. So you see, smoking can be good for you.'

Denise Welch: Actress

'I feel like a right hypocrite because I caught my fifteen-year-old son smoking recently and I was very disappointed. However, I'm afraid it's "Do as I say" not "Do as I do" in the family home. I always love a cigarette before going down the red carpet at a showbiz do. It can be quite daunting, wondering why people are waving, shouting your name and asking for autographs. One minute it seems I'm just a normal stay-at-home mum sorting out my youngest son's dinner or checking the eldest has done his homework. Next I'm being feted and treated like royalty. No matter how many times I go to a showbiz bash I don't think I'll ever get used to the adulation.

'Once, at a Children in Crisis charity event, I agreed to model a dress by designer Isabell Kristiansen, who was hosting the evening. I got to the venue, the exclusive Cafe Royal in London, and came face to face with the other models. An intimidating collection of gorgeous, leggy models with minuscule hips and tiny waists. One of them was Jerry Hall. Petrified doesn't come into it, and to make matters worse I was to model a £4,000 dress. No way would I have risked smoking in a gown like that. Everyone was so kind and I had a great time. But once the show was over that dress came off immediately and I went straight for a fag. Boy, did it taste good. Like everything, when you can't have it, the more you want it.'

Sophie Anderton: Model

'Last year I was in the TV reality show *I'm A Celebrity Get Me Out Of Here*, which was filmed in Australia. It was great, and would have been totally hellish without cigarettes. I'd like to say the best smoke of my life was the one I had after eating live bugs in my hideous bushtucker trial. Certainly it helped to get rid of the taste and took my mind off what had been a truly revolting experience. But always the most glorious cigarette is the one after a long-haul flight. Crossing the Atlantic without a puff can be a real killer, especially when you discover you've landed in an airport with a po-faced "no-smoking inside the building" policy. I can still remember the sensation, after the 24-hour flight to Australia, of lighting up and feeling a sense of calm wash over me. All my fear and trepidation of what lay ahead in the jungle disappeared momentarily. A smoker's relationship with a cigarette is very intimate, it can block the rest of the world out. I love it.'

France Zeffirelli: Film Director

'Cigarettes are my muse, my way of reflecting and my great companion. I've smoked since I was nine and have never worked without them. In 1977, when working at the Vienna Opera, I had a contract which gave me special dispensation to smoke. Surrounded by "Rauchen Verboten" signs I was followed everywhere by two firemen, one with a bucket of sand, the other with a bucket of water.

My most memorable, however, was when I was flying from New York to London on TWA at the beginning of the new tobacco ban on planes. I always feel tense flying and needed the comfort of my good friend and support, so eventually I went to the rest room and lit a cigarette. A forbidden smoke is quite an exhilarating experience. Then I stepped outside to find an American lady waiting to use the loo. She called the attendant and had me dragged back to the scene of the crime, where she screamed at me for violating the clean-air policy of the airline. I told her, "Me. I never would have done that." But she kept on haranguing me until at last I said, "Madame, I am terribly sorry in that even my shit smells of smoke."'

Jilly Johnson: Model/Actress

'My all-time favourite cigarette was after my first theatre performance in *Funny Peculiar* at the Mermaid Theatre in London. I was the saucy love interest opposite Peter Duncan; the whole cast was very experienced and it was my first big part with loads of dialogue. It was challenging but very frightening. I was dying for a cigarette before I went on to calm my nerves but there were loads of love scenes and the smell of tobacco on one's breath is hardly polite. After the curtain went down, and I'd managed not to fluff my lines, I lit up a Silk Cut. I can remember the feeling vividly. It felt like a nice comfort blanket reassuring me that I'd done all right on the night.'

Nicola Duffet: Actress

'I'm not afraid to say that I had the odd cigarette when I was pregnant with my nine-year-old daughter Poppy. It kept me sane. But it was nothing like my normal consumption of about twenty a day. I opted for natural childbirth and, in hindsight, I think I must have been out of my mind. They had to tie me down, quite literally. To say it was the most pain I'd ever experienced is an understatement. Between using language a lady should never use, I was screaming: "Give me a bloody cigarette." After

I'd given birth to my beautiful bundle of joy, I was told to rest for six hours before moving from the bed. Not being a girl who ever does as she's told I was up after four hours, in the car park and puffing away on a cigarette that felt like pure gold.'

Sarah Lancashire: Actress

'It was Christmas 1999 and I'd given up smoking for six months. I put the turkey in the oven then realised I hadn't taken the giblets out. They were in a plastic bag somewhere. I had to take out the turkey, take out the stuffing and shove my hand up its bottom. I felt like such a failure. I was in tears. Then my brother came in with a packet of Silk Cut and that was that. It was lovely.'

Anthony Worrall Thomson: Chef

'I'd just run my first marathon and had given up smoking for six weeks prior to the big day. I walked into The Savoy Hotel as a guest of Anton Edelmann, totally exhausted but exhilarated after the race. The first thing I did was to light up … and promptly keel over. I fainted. I was completely out of it until ten the next morning having suffered no pain, discomfort or aches whatsoever. And I got a room at The Savoy for free. Fantastic.'

Jeremy Clarkson: Top Gear Presenter and Columnist

'It has to be on a chairlift, having just completed a tricky ski run at Val d'Isere. There's something about the juxtaposition of ingesting hydrochloric acid – or whatever chemical it is they put in cigarettes – in one of the crispest, healthiest environments in the world. You're surrounded by this superb Alpine vista, you're on your own, you look beneath you and think, I just skied down that, I've *earned* this cigarette. It's like, "look at all this good around me and the harm I'm doing." No smoke on earth can get better than that.'

Shane Richie: Eastenders Star

'It was the day my son Shane junior was born. I wasn't much of a smoker at the time but my wife, Colleen, was and after what she'd been through felt desperate for a cigarette. "Don't worry," I told her, "I'll have one for you."

"Oh, go on then," she said.

So I went outside and I swear it was the best smoke I've ever had. First, there was the head rush from the birth of Shane junior, followed quickly by the one I got from that cigarette.'

Daniella Westbrook: Actress

'There have been so many times I've enjoyed a cigarette, it's hard to pin-point one. It's been well documented that I've been in rehab and, though I wanted to give up smoking, my therapist told me it would be unrealistic for me to give up everything at once. However, when I had cosmetic surgery there was no choice. Smoking thins the blood, making the healing process more difficult, so I was forced to stop. I was back on them after my surgery, but when my son told me that if I gave up it would be his best present ever my heart jumped. I enrolled at the famous Allen Carr school the next week.

Carr is a guru in his field and his promise that he can cure you of smoking in one day has worked for so many people. As I stood in the school doorway on a wet rainy day in darkest Wimbledon and lit what I thought was going to be my last cigarette, I felt like I was saying goodbye to an old friend. I learned when I was inside the school that you could smoke all day until leaving – it was a bit like being in therapy except there was a fog of smoke. It works for many but to me it felt like I was being brainwashed. And not very successfully ... that night I sat down to watch TV and lit up!'

Nicola Wheeler: Emmerdale Actress

'I smoke primarily when I'm stressed and definitely this was the case when I appeared on *Celebrities Under Pressure*. I had to live with a lovely family for seven days while learning to juggle 13 cigar boxes. After the week was up I had to go to the studio, perform the juggling act in front of a live studio audience and get it exactly right in order for the family to win the terrific prizes. Easy, eh? To say I was petrified is an understatement. I texted all my friends asking them to send out great vibes at 7pm that evening. I came off and went straight to my handbag and out with my fags. I was never so glad to smoke a cig in my life.'

Simon Cowell: Pop Idol Star

'About ten years ago, when everyone was going on about giving up smoking, I booked myself, reluctantly, into a hypnotherapist. I waited, bored out of my mind in his Harley Street surgery, before going through this charade of pretending to be hypnotised. All I could think about was getting outside and lighting up, which I did immediately. I can remember racing out and enjoying that cigarette like it was the best ever.

The next best has to be the one on the pavement at Los Angeles Airport after I've run through customs. Comparable to that is sitting on a chairlift after skiing. Working in TV studios has never stopped me smoking. Once, during my second year on *American Idol*, I was asked by a major entertainment company if I'd present a show. I wasn't particularly interested but they pestered and pestered me until, finally, I said, 'Okay, I'll do it if you let me smoke throughout my presentation.' They agreed and the show went out all over America with me smoking constantly. And do you know, there was not one single complaint.'

CHAPTER ELEVEN

POSTSCRIPT: THERE OUGHT NOT TO BE A LAW

Sorry, it's my last one

'Any law that inspires disrespect for other laws – the good laws – is a bad law.'

Calvin Coolidge (Thirtieth President
of the United States 1923-29)

And so we say our goodbyes, with the gloomy prospect of a draconian smoking ban in restaurants, pubs and bars not far off. Of course, there's always the problem of who is going to manhandle the octogenarian war veteran and his Dunhill out of the snug bar into the driving rain, but undoubtedly some officious little busybody will be on hand to oblige.

But all is not lost. A quick leaf through *The Joy of Smoking* reminds you that we've been here before. Anti-smokers have been around for as long as the weed, but it's survived and thrived, and is still here to tell its fascinating tale.

The origins of tobacco may never be known. Five hundred years ago tobacco had never been seen, felt, or thought of by any outside the Americas, yet today it is grown in 120 countries throughout the world and there is not a single country where smoking is not part of everyday life. Despite the efforts of the anti-smokers, over one billion people smoke 5.5 trillion cigarettes annually, the country boasting the greatest number being China, with 340 million smokers.

In August 1997, Jeanne Calment died in Arles, France, at the age of 122. She was not only the world's oldest person, but the world's oldest smoker – and she had the birth certificate to prove it. As Sir Walter Raleigh languished in prison, the father of British smoking inscribed on his pipe box, 'It was my companion in that most wretched time'. To Sir Walter and Jeanne Calment, and millions of smokers in between, tobacco has been a relaxation, a comfort, an inspiration … and a friend.